BREAKING INTO SPIRITUAL PRISONS

TAKING BACK WHAT IS RIGHTFULLY YOURS

Ramón Saenz

OUT OF DARKNESS MINISTRIES
PUBLICATIONS
ADRIAN, MICHIGAN

Breaking into Spiritual Prisons
Ramón Saenz
First Edition

Published by:
    Out of Darkness Ministries
    Publications
    Post Office Box 591
    Adrian, MI 49221-9810 U.S.A.

Copyright © 1998 by Ramón Saenz

All rights reserved. No part of this book may be reproduced or transmitted in any form or by any means, electronic or mechanical, including photocopying, recording or by any information storage and retrieval system without written permission from the author, except for the inclusion of brief quotations in a review.

First Printing 1998

Unless otherwise noted, the Bible version used in this publication is the *Spirit Filled Life Bible*, New King James Version, Copyright Thomas Nelson, Inc., 1983. Used by permission.

Unless otherwise noted, the definitions given in this book are used "By permission. From The Merriam-Webster Dictionary, Copyright © 1994 by Merriam-Webster Inc."

Publisher's Cataloging in Publication
(Provided by Quality Books, Inc.)

Saenz, Ramon (Ramon O.) 1945–
    Breaking into spiritual prisons / Ramon Saenz. — 1st ed.

    p. cm.
    Preassigned LCCN: 97-92467
    ISBN 1-892125-24-2

    1. Conversion. 2. Saenz, Ramon (Ramon O.) 1945–
    3. Converts. 4. Spiritual biography. I. Title.

BV4921.2.S34 1998   248 2'46
                                      QBI98-356

Printed in the United States of America
at Morgan Printing in Austin, Texas

DEDICATION

This book is lovingly dedicated to my wife, Gloria, and to our three children, Sonya, Tina, and Vicente, who literally went through a hell of their own until their prayers where finally answered. I thank them for their unending faith and support, and I believe that it was because of their prayers, along with the prayers of many others, that God heard my cry.

Contents

About the Author 7
Acknowledgments 11
Introduction 13
1. The Battle Cries 17
2. The Journey Begins 28
3. The Road Ahead 40
4. A New Understanding 51
5. First Things First 63
6. The Plan: Know that There Is One! 78
7. Facing the Music 90
8. Exposing the Enemy 102
9. The Promised Land 118
10. You Are Right Where You Are Supposed to Be 133
11. It Really Does Matter 145
12. Dare to Begin 157
13. Paid for by the Blood 172
14. Stay in the Father's House 188
15. The Storm Is Passing By 200
16. Out of Darkness into His Marvelous Light 211
17. Today Really Is Your Day 222

About the Author

Ramón Saenz had no idea what awaited him after being taken from a life of alcohol, drugs, violence, and abusive behavior on July 1, 1992. That which the world had introduced to him and that had become his reason for living had now been shattered, leaving Ramón to look ahead into a future with absolutely no understanding of what was happening to him. Nevertheless, he welcomed the internal release from all he had come to know during the previous forty six years—with no comprehension as to why, other than that he was finally experiencing peace, something that had evaded him most of his life.

Born September 14, 1945, in Adrian, Michigan, to Vicente Saenz and María Torres Saenz, Ramón was one of seven children and continues to make his home in Adrian, a small city in Lenawee County in southeastern Michigan. Having attended different schools in the county, he finally graduated from Tecumseh High School in 1963. He then attended Jackson Business University for a very short time, but his tenure there came to an abrupt end after one too many problems with the law. This was to be the end of his formal education.

The course of Ramón's tumultuous and chaotic lifestyle had been marked by the premature death of his father when Ramón was eight years old. His father's death created a very early prison in Ramón's life—a prison filled with hatred, anger, bitterness, and revenge. These internal storms led him to alcohol, drug abuse, gang activity, and—ultimately—incarceration, not only within himself, but in a number of correctional institutions. It was at the age of twenty-six that Ramón finally reached a point that started him in a different direction.

Entering into a relationship with Gloria García in the summer of 1971, he proposed and was married to her on February 26, 1972. This marriage brought them two daughters and one son over the next seven years.

Unfortunately though, the bondage that Ramón had known for most of his early life almost immediately began to reclaim his attention. This created a very turbulent married life, not only for him but for the members of his immediate family. Now even they were being exposed to the anger, the bitterness, the revenge, and the hatred which had him bound within his inner being, and now even they were being unwillingly led into a life of alcohol and drugs. For the next twenty years, they would be on an emotional rollercoaster, watching as their husband and father slowly progressed toward destruction. Watching as the nightmare slowly led him to ride the train to its end, as it had his brother, who had been a year younger, and who had committed suicide in 1980.

But at last the cries came and someone heard. The pain, the hurt, and the suffering had become so unbearable that it finally caused him to cry out to a God in whom he had never believed, and He had heard his cries.

With absolutely no idea what was in store for him that first day of July, 1992, Ramón was being taken on a journey that would ultimately birth a ministry committed to reaching those who were trapped in spiritual prisons of their own, as he had been; committed to exposing the weapons that were being used to keep people imprisoned within themselves; committed to exposing the truth about just what exactly was being done by Satan to keep one locked in the deepest part of the dungeon of the spiritual prison within. Becoming licensed to preach the gospel, Ramón soon found himself heading an outreach ministry that would take him back to the man-made prisons and to churches of different denominations to share what Jesus Christ had done for him.

Today, Ramón heads the Out of Darkness Ministries, which has been expanded to reach thousands who are trapped within the toughest prison there is—the spiritual prison within. Having added a Publications Department to the ministries in 1997, Ramón now looks to reaching millions under the direction of the One who called him out of darkness into His Marvelous Light, Jesus Christ.

Acknowledgments

First and foremost, I give the glory and honor to Jesus Christ for having brought me out of the darkness which had prevailed in my life, for without Him this book would not have been possible.

I have not attempted to cite in the text all the authorities and sources consulted in the preparation of this book. To do so would require more space than is available. The list would include a great number of family members, coworkers, and many, many other friends, but mention must be made of some.

I sincerely am grateful to my pastors, Pete and Shirley Valdéz, for their continuous support as I battled through the walls which stood before me.

I sincerely am grateful to my friends Frank and Dottie Norman who were always there to encourage me, and especially to Frank who was like a brother to me and who would continuously remind me to stand still and to wait on the Lord.

I sincerely am grateful to my friends Ted Griffin, Debbie Holtz, Ron Kidman, Arjela Marsh, Linda Miller, Bonnie Null, Renee Stewart, Sandy Vanderpool, and Lisa Waggoner, all who served as much-needed reviewers, critics, and/or supporters as I wrote.

I sincerely thank all these fine people. I know they are as proud of the part they have played in the development of this book as they are of their contribution to this work.

I also would like to extend my appreciation to Dan Poynter whose book, *The Self-Publishing Manual*, assisted in the development of the Publications Department of our ministries.

Copyediting by Nancy Meredith

Book design by Terry Sherrell

Cover design by Stephen Bright
and Ted M. Griffin

Introduction

The title "Breaking into Spiritual Prisons" seemed odd at first, but as I began to look back over the past few years, beginning with the day I experienced a complete transformation in my life, I realized that this is exactly what must happen if one is to experience true freedom. For me, there had to be a literal breaking into the person I had been on the inside, if I was ever to know the real answer to why I did the things I so desperately did not want to do.

For most of my adult life, I was plagued with absolute confusion and torment, not being able to understand what was going on until it was almost too late. The memories still come back when I give thought to just how trapped I had really been, how I had literally shut myself off from the rest of the world. My life was being destroyed without my having any awareness of it. Many times I had mentally beat myself up for what I had done the night before, and many times I had felt the fear that comes from being unable to recall what I had done. None of this made any sense to me. I actually thought that I was going crazy.

All I knew was, that of the times that I could remember, I always ended up doing something I knew I should not be doing.

It was all so puzzling to me; here I was, supposedly an adult, with no control of what I did. My life was getting out of hand, for even though I wanted so desperately not to do those things, I could not stop myself.

The days passed, and as they slowly turned into years, I knew that I was becoming progressively worse. I had reached the point where I had absolutely no priorities in my life anymore, other than to continue to alienate myself from those who truly loved me, as they endured the pain of watching me destroy myself. They were unable to do anything about it but pray.

Without realizing it, I had been on a mission to shut off all ties that I had with life. I was withdrawing from life. I knew I was alive, but was I really? I was heading into total darkness.

What happened to me next revealed the answers I had been searching for, for what seems to be my entire life. It was the first day of July,1992, that my spiritual prison was broken, and what happened that day was the beginning of a brand new life for me.

Since that fateful day I have gained more and more understanding about the importance of breaking into inner prisons as a way to truly have a chance of surviving and of finding inner peace. As I read about all the suicides and vicious murders that are happening at an alarming rate, I am deeply saddened. The majority of these lives are ending with absolutely no reason. No one can understand why. One of those deaths could have been mine if I hadn't found a different way.

Today I look at my life with great expectations and excitement. This is something that is completely different for me. The excitement that I am feeling is so real that I can no longer confine the joy to myself and the small nucleus of people involved in my life today. I am guided to begin expanding from the few hundred people I minister to in different areas and who have become a part of my life, to the thousands of people I know are trapped in the same type of internal prison I had been in, and many who are absolutely unaware of it.

I write with the belief and confidence that as you read this book, the same awesome power which came to set me free from inner bondage will also come upon you. Just as it was for me, it is time for the darkness to be lifted from your life, for the lies to be exposed, and for the truth to be brought forth. You, too, will understand why breaking into your own prison is so important in finding out just who you are.

As you go forth on your journey, I can assure you that you will truly find it to have been well worth the effort.

◄ Today Is Your Day! ►

~ 1 ~

THE BATTLE CRIES

I felt the warmth from the sun on my face as it stirred me from a deep, deep sleep. It felt so good as I lay there on the floor... then I opened my eyes as fear completely overtook my entire being. *Oh my God, what have I done? Where have I been? Why am I sleeping on the floor? Where is everyone?*

I tried getting up, unsuccessfully. I felt completely nauseated and my head was pounding terribly. *What is wrong with me?* Here I was on the floor again, where it seemed I would always land, as I somehow tried to make it to the bedroom in the dark.

Why couldn't I just go out and act like everyone else? Why couldn't I just stop? Why was I allowing all of this to happen to me? I knew better. I always knew better. The drunken nights, the battle with drugs, the abuse I put my wife and children through every night I went out, the continuous fights, the name calling, the false accusations I made, the torment I was putting my family through, the torment I was putting myself through... when would all this hell come to an end? When would the confusion just stop? When would I start doing those things that I really wanted to do, and stop doing those things that I so desperately did not want to do? Why was I not able to stop? When would the nightmare end? When would all of this hell just cease to exist?

My head hurt so much that I couldn't think straight. My entire being was filled with that same ugly, tormenting fear that I had known so many times before. My whole body was shaking, and I couldn't stop. *Oh God, please help me!*

I knew I had to get up. *Just where is everybody?* If I was lucky, maybe they had all left for school and for work already, and I wouldn't get yelled at again. I just couldn't take that right now. *Why do they always have to yell anyway?* They just don't understand what I'm going through.

Just what was it that I really was going through? I didn't even remember where I had gone or what I had done. I couldn't even remember what day it was, nor what time.

Oh, my God, did they really leave me this time? How much more will they take? I love them so much! I have such a beautiful wife and three fantastic children. Why can't I just stop, at least for them? What is wrong with me?

I was on my back, and my head began to spin as I attempted to get up. I decided that it would be better if I just rolled over. It would be easier to just crawl. *Where is everybody? Please God, don't let them have really left this time. I promise that I will not let this happen again. What will I do if they leave me?*

I started to crawl to the bathroom and reached for the sink to help myself up. I was so stupid. Where had I been? What day was it today? My God, what had happened to me?

I was kneeling against the sink and it came to me that I had been at work the night before, and that I had been sent home. But... what, exactly, had I done? I couldn't remember. It just wouldn't come to me. I needed to get up. I needed to get straight. I began pulling myself up and could see myself in the mirror as I unsteadily tried to hang on to avoid falling back.

Who was that ugly person I was staring at in the mirror? What was wrong with him? He looked like some kind of monster. *It couldn't be me. My God, help me. Please help me to end this torment. Help me to end this pain. I don't want to live like this *anymore. Why can't I just stop? I am so sick and tired of being like this. I am just so tired!*

The warmth of my tears began to stir me back to reality. What had happened? Why was I on the floor again? How long had I been sitting here crying? It felt good, though. What a warm feeling I had inside! My head had stopped pounding. It didn't hurt anymore. Nor was I feeling nausea. What had just happened to me?

As I tried to remember what I had been doing, I recalled that I had been looking at myself in the mirror and that I had hated what I had been looking at. The image I had seen was very, very ugly. I had been staring at a distorted and miserable person. I recall even trying to erase the image in the mirror as if it had been an illusion. I just wanted the image to go away. I didn't want to see it anymore. I was tired of looking at that person. I didn't want to see that face anymore.

I remember that I had started to scream at the mirror as tears began to cloud my vision. I had started to get dizzy, and the image in the mirror was growing distant. I remember starting to call out to God. *My God, if you are for real, if this Jesus Christ is for real, I beg you to please take this hurt that I am feeling right now away. Please take away this pain, this suffering. Please help me to stop drinking, to stop using drugs. Please remove all of this from me. Please God, just help me to get better. Please God, please.*

I remember asking myself, who was I kidding? How many more times was I going to keep telling these lies? I knew that I had prayed to this God each and every time I felt like this. It was becoming a regular ritual for me. I didn't deserve to have God make me feel better, if there really was one. I knew that I would be feeling like this again. What was I praying for? I knew that the only reason that I even prayed at all was because my parents always did. They always prayed.

The name of Jesus Christ must have come along some time while I was growing up. Maybe it was during the time when I served as an altar boy, or had attended a Catholic school. Or possibly I had picked it up during one of my rare visits to church on a Sunday. I really don't know, but I do know that it was a long time ago.

I was merely copying what my parents always used to do. Pray! I do know, though, that my prayers were always said when I was either drunk, had done something wrong, was in some kind of trouble, or was simply in jail. My prayers would always be the same: *God, if you will only help me out of this one, I'll never do it again*, knowing that I would be doing it again sometime. What a joke I had been. I never really did believe in God, or in this person called Jesus Christ. I knew that it had been just a formality on my part... just in case.

I was feeling very, very weak, as if all my strength had just left me. The tears continued to fall and I felt helpless. What was I going to do?

God, I am so very, very sorry. If you truly are for real, and Jesus is also for real, I ask for Your forgiveness. Forgive me for all that I have done, for all the hurt that I have caused, for what I have done to my family, for the lies and the damage that I have caused in their lives, for not having believed in You. Oh God, I do not deserve to live anymore. Oh, God, just please forgive me.

My thoughts were beginning to come back. How long had I been sitting there? What had happened to me? It was such a warm, wonderful feeling that I was experiencing at that very moment as I sat there on the floor. Somehow, I knew that I would never hurt ever again. I knew that I would never taste another drop of alcohol again, or use another drug again. Somehow, I knew that I would never hate again, or feel fear again. Somehow, I knew that I would never go down this road ever again!

For some strange reason, I felt as if everything had been lifted from me, and I somehow knew that this person, this Jesus Christ to whom I had cried out, had somehow had something to do with this transformation. He had come to set me free. Somehow, everything within me wanted to jump for joy! My whole inner being felt as if it were ready to jump out. I had just experienced something I had never felt before, and that I could not understand., but I didn't care. I felt so good. I felt so free. I was actually feeling like a new person!

At that very moment, I realized that Jesus Christ had made His Presence known to me. He had come to let me know that, in fact, He was for real. I made up my mind right then and there that I was going to follow Him, no matter what, that I was going to serve this absolutely awesome God who had just given me a new life.

What a newfound freedom I was experiencing. It was a feeling that I had never known before in my life. Even in my so called 'best' days, I could not recall one day that I had ever felt this good. Though I could not explain it, I had been set free from all the things that had held me trapped for so very, very long. I had been released from a prison where I was held a prisoner for the majority of my life, not even knowing it.

I was determined to search for information that would lead me to know just who Jesus Christ was. No matter what I had to do, no matter what I had to go through, I was going to get to know Him. I was ever so grateful that the fears, the angers, the bitterness, the hatreds, the desire for alcohol and drugs, had all at once been lifted from me. In my innermost being, I knew that they were gone forever. I just knew. I didn't know how, but I just knew.

This relief is something that I had been attempting to achieve on my own for so very long. I needed to know this person who was able to lift all of my burden from me in just one day! What was it about Him and His awesome power, that He was suddenly able to make everything better? I was determined to find out!

As I slowly started to get up from the floor, I felt like a totally different person. I had such a peace within me. I knew that it was still me, but somehow, I was different. I did not feel the fear that I had become accustomed to feeling. I did not feel the anxiety that I used to feel, wondering what was going to be said to me.

After I had gotten up, it came to me that the date was July 1, 1992, and I knew that I would forever remember this date. It was the beginning of a new life, the beginning of a new person. I was so very, very excited. What a joy I was feeling inside! For the first time I could remember, I felt truly alive. What a glorious moment! What a glorious day! I couldn't wait to tell my wife and kids. They were going to be so happy. Finally, I was really going to be all right. And then, reality hit!

Somewhere amidst all of the joy and excitement, even though I knew deep down inside that I would never return to the hell that I had just come from, my thoughts were directed to a truth that suddenly came upon me. *No one is going to believe me!* It was then that I discovered there had truly been a change in the person I had been. I discovered instantly that I did not fall to pieces. I was not overcome with panic. My thoughts did not instantly turn to fear, but instead I found myself saying, *why should they believe? Just why should my wife believe me? Why should she believe me after twenty years of nothing but letdowns? Why should my children believe me after all the mental abuse and torment they have gone through?*

What a time of awakening I was having! It was great. It was just great! I mean, I was not even torn up about it as I normally would have been. This was just great!

Hadn't I made promises before that things were going to be better? How many times had I stopped drinking, pretending to be better? How many times had I pretended to have my act together just to return a short time later to the misery, the abuse, the anger, the lies, the false accusations? Why should they believe? Why should anyone believe me? I could hear their words already: *I've heard that one before, when are you going back?*

My wife and children were desperately trying to love and understand me, and I knew that deep down inside. But I also knew that they were losing hope. Day after day. Year after year. Lie after lie. Broken promise after broken promise. Why should they believe what had just happened to me?

What a glorious day was July 1, 1992! There had been something so special about it that not even the thought of my loved ones not believing me could destroy the excitement and the joy I was feeling.

The peace, the joy, the excitement that I had just received was assuring me that it just did not make any difference. It just did not matter whether anyone ever believed me or not. I knew! Yes, I knew that something great and awesome had just happened in my life!

I did not understand, nor could I begin to explain, but somehow this person named Jesus Christ had just spoken to me. I knew that I had been set free, and it was He who was assuring me that all would be taken care of, and that I would be okay. It was He who had assured me that I would hurt no more.

It had been Jesus Christ whom I had heard say to me that He would lead the way, and all I needed to do was follow Him. It was He who said to me that He would protect me, and that, therefore, I need not be concerned about what others would say or think, that it didn't make any difference whether they believed me or not, for, in time, He would take care of even that situation. I felt so wonderful. It felt so good to be alive.

A New Day

My thirteen-month-old great-nephew, Travón, had just passed away. It was August 22, 1996, and I was beginning to experience a truly grieving spirit for the number of God's children who were being taken away because of the evil that was becoming so prominent in their lives.

It had been a little over four years since Christ had come to set me free from the prison where I had been bound. It was the very next day after Travón's death, that Jesus placed within my heart the knowledge that the time had come to begin doing what He had truly called me to do.

From the very beginning I had wanted to share what He had done for me. I had begun seeking the truth almost immediately. In fact, I started looking for a Bible I had had before, and after having located it, I immediately started to read. I had such a hunger within me to know more about this Jesus that all I could think of doing was to read.

I had thought it a shame for me to keep my experience within myself, and I knew that the day would come when I would begin to share it with others. It seemed unfair for me to feel the joy and excitement that I was feeling while I watching others being destroyed. Not knowing exactly what I would do, nor how I would bring this across, I simply believed that if Jesus had been able to take all of the hurts and pains I had been experiencing in my life away, then I knew that He would show me what I had to do.

My work first began in His Word. I felt an excitement from the very start, as I began to explore His Word—something I had never known before. There was a hunger inside of me, a driving force, as I continued to read. I felt like a sponge, wanting to absorb more and more.

Not quite a month had passed since my experience with Christ and daily reading of His Word at my kitchen table. I felt an urge to just begin. Somehow, I knew this urge had been placed there by Christ, and He was telling me it was time. That was more than enough for me. I was ready to go. This was what I had been waiting for. Within me, I knew that Jesus was truly leading the way, and I but needed to follow. Somehow, I knew that all I had to do was show up, and He would do the rest. All I had to do was be still, listen, and be obedient to whatever He told me to do.

I was truly excited! I was hearing His voice within me! His words were coming true in my life. He had promised me that He would lead the way, and He was doing just that. My first time out I went to a place I had visited many times before. This place had been a haven for me over the past twelve years, for it was a place where others who were experiencing the same outer problems would come together—Alcoholics Anonymous. I was familiar with the procedures of the program, so it was an easy transition for me; I felt that this was where I should be. At first my journey didn't offer me many open doors, but then I really didn't know what doors I had expected to be open. Somehow though, I felt that something would happen.

It was hard to imagine the things I was going to learn during the years to come or the changes that were going to be made within me. One very important change was the knowledge that alcohol and drugs were merely superficial coverups for even greater problems. I began working with others who were bound outwardly with alcohol and drugs. I say outwardly, for I knew that the real culprit is not alcohol or drugs, but the prison in which we are bound within ourselves.

This was the truth I had to share with others. They had to realize that they did not have to end up in the horrible way that destruction was leading them. They had to know that there was another way. They had to know who the real enemy was and what his plan was for them in their life. The enemy had to be exposed.

Alcohol and drugs had created such an illusion in my mind that I had focused on them as the major problem in my life while covering up the real issues that were holding me in bondage. In reality, alcohol and drugs were merely the obstacles and weapons that were chosen to create the smoke screen that would keep me from ever focusing on the real enemy. That enemy had continued to grow stronger for as long as I remained in the smoke screen, unaware of its destructive force in my life.

That force had kept me bound behind the walls that had gotten thicker with every year that went by. That force had kept me bound in the darkness, in the deepest part of its dungeons, as it grew even more intense with every single day that passed. That force had taken me so far down into its depths that I had already begun to desire to escape the nightmare.

Fortunately, the enemy had missed one important piece of information. Not only did the enemy have a plan for my life, but so did Jesus! I am so thankful that I had reached the point of having nowhere else to turn, for it was having my back up against the wall that forced me to cry out to Him. Yes, Jesus had a plan!

I was intrigued after having discovered that alcohol and drugs were only coverups and smoke screens for something deeper. Even those who did not drink or use drugs were caught up in the same prisons within as I had been. Many were caught up in feelings that involved their careers, their bosses, their spouses, their children, their finances, their circumstances, just to name a few. These outward manifestations were seen as the major problems in life, which led them to seek outside assistance. This is exactly what the enemy is hoping will happen! For as long as we continue to look at outward conflicts as the major problem, it will never cross our minds to look into the inner core of our beings, and as long as we do not look into the inner core, we will never know the truth of who the true enemy really is.

I assure you, the real enemy is not you. It is not the alcohol. It is not the drugs. It is not the spouses. It is not the children. It is not the finances. It is not the circumstances we find ourselves in. It is not anything we might be looking at that causes us to place the blame on ourselves. All of these, along with many, many more, are the weapons used to divert our attention from the real enemy. Think about it. If you were my enemy, would you expose your plans to me so that I might prepare myself to do battle against you, or would you attempt to divert my attention to other things so that I would not see you coming?

The answer should be quite obvious, and likewise, the real enemy is not going to let you see who he is until it is too late, like it almost was for me. He will keep you off guard until he is able to destroy you, like he almost destroyed me. Today I look past all of the smoke. I look past all of the outward appearances. I look past all that the world would say is the problem and look directly to the inner core of the person. Today I know who the real enemy is, and I go directly after him in order to expose him. The troubled person is not the problem. People are lied to, tricked into placing the blame upon themselves. This is why it is so important that they know the truth. Today I know there must be a breakthrough if one is to be set at liberty. There must be a deliverance from all of these weapons if one is to know freedom.

Until every weapon that is formed and used against you to keep you imprisoned within yourself is destroyed, captivity will prevail, but how could you be aware of this, if it is never exposed in your life? How could you know that your divorce did not happen just because there was no more love, or because there was no more spark in your marriage, or because you just could not stand to be with each other anymore? How could you know that the stress did not come about just because of the children, or because of your spouse, or because you worked too much, or because the bills got too out of hand, or because of this, or because of that?

My purpose for writing this book is to help you go beyond the weapons that are being used against you, for the weapons I refer to are those that have been destroyed in my own life. Today I am able to see through all the exterior weapons that have been formed against people, because they had such a powerful effect on me. Because of the destruction of these weapons, I can see clearly now how I was held captive for all of those years.

I will write more in depth on this matter in a later chapter, but for now, know that what seems to be a problem is not always the problem. More often than not, the reasons are more deeply rooted than what is being displayed on the surface, which is exactly what *Breaking into Spiritual Prisons* is all about.

All I ask of you at this point is that you not attempt to figure it out beforehand. Do not attempt to analyze what is being said, but simply receive it. It will all be made clear as you go along. I say this, for I have come to know numerous tricks that the enemy uses to keep us from knowing the truth about him. The temptation to analyze before the whole message is received is only an attempt to divert your attention. Do not allow the enemy, who has already brought about so much chaos and destruction in our world, to trick you into the "I know" trap. It is so crucial for you to give yourself the opportunity to know the truth.

Having been set free from the ugly, dark, cold, dreary, and isolated inner prison where I had been held captive for so many, many years without my having any knowledge of it, I now feel driven to begin exposing the things that were behind those walls, to begin exposing those things that are kept hidden from us to keep us from ever knowing the truth.

I truly believe that Jesus had a plan for me. This includes what I am doing today—exposing the enemy for what and who he is. I am more than ready to do it! It is not necessary that you believe these words at this time, but I assure you, that as you continue to read, the truth will be made known to your inner being. You will know it, for you will feel it.

> Happy is the man who finds wisdom, and the man who gains understanding. For her proceeds are better than the profits of silver, and gain than fine gold.
> (Proverbs 3:13-14)

◄ Today Is Your Day! ►

~2~

The Journey Begins

For almost two solid years, I attended AA meetings every single day. I was not new to the program, as I had been in and out of AA for the past twelve years, trying to get my life back in order. This time, though, my experience seemed completely different.

From the very first day I started back into AA, there was an indescribable excitement that filled my entire being because of what had happened to me just a little over thirty days previously. This excitement grew even more intense as the days passed.

Every single day, every single meeting, every single person had become a new challenge in my life, challenging me to become an even better person than I had been the day before.

My first year passed by very quickly. I was a new person, blessed with a new life, and I was experiencing many new and wondrous things that somehow I had missed when I was caught up in my old life. I refer to just the simple things in life, like the trees, the stars, the sky—even the sunlight seemed to be brighter. I remember the fall of 1993, a little over one year after the change in my life, when I made a comment to my wife about the beautiful colors in the trees. I recall the look that she gave me, as if to say, "where have you been all your life?" These were some of the wonderful things I had missed before.

I was finding out many new things about myself, things I had come to accept that I would eventually have to confront if I wanted to grow even more, but even these changes were great, because it still was all so very new to me. I knew that I would be able to depend on Jesus Christ, who had already taken me through so much, to lead me in the way that He had called me to go, to prepare me to do His work, to confront and defeat the obstacles that He had told me I would be challenged with as I moved forward.

By the end of my first year in my new life (which is exactly what I felt it was) I found that I wasn't as open as I thought I would have been. The joy and the excitement that I had experienced that first day were still very evident in my life, but somehow I was caught up by the fact that I was referring to this awesome, wonderful, and spectacular God who had just performed a miracle in my life only as "the God of my own understanding." Still, I was okay with that for the time.

I continued to read God's word faithfully every day. It seemed that I could never get enough. I was spending anywhere from two to three hours daily searching through His scriptures. This reading not only sustained the joy and excitement I had received, but it was teaching me to look through many things that I normally would not have been able to look through.

I had been confronted with many challenges that first year, requiring me to search way into my being just to find the strength to get through them, but as with all my problems, I looked to the One who had pulled me through even greater trials, Jesus Christ.

As I began my second year in the program, I received a new burst of energy. I felt the best that I had ever felt. I was now approaching my forty-eighth birthday, and I felt completely renewed. I was alive, and my life had definitely taken a turn for the better.

I was still attending meetings daily, and the joy I had known was growing even more. The excitement that I had felt that first year seemed now to have doubled, and I was loving every minute of it. What a glorious way to live one's life. What a change from where I had been just a little over a year before! I couldn't wait to share it with others, in hopes that they too, would know what true freedom really is.

This new vigor and energy was bringing me to heights I had never known before. I found myself sharing my experience at the meetings, just like it had been that very first day. But now, I was giving all the glory to Jesus Christ. I spoke at meetings with an even greater enthusiasm about the person who had set me free. I spoke of Jesus Christ. Many were becoming attracted to what I was sharing with them. Many asked for more. With every day and every meeting that passed, I grew even more enthusiastic and determined to share.

The period shortly after Christmas of 1993 was a joyous time for me. My life was ever so exciting, and this Christmas had been even better than the last. Jesus was truly alive in my person. I had a peace within me at depths that I had never known. I can honestly say that the love I felt for my wife and children was greater than I had never known. I had such a love for all those with whom I came in contact. I was so excited!

There had even been an additional blessing in my life. Almost two months earlier, I had been set free of yet another bondage that had reigned in my life for nearly thirty-two years. It was about eleven-thirty at night on November 7, 1993. I was lying in bed watching a gospel program on television, and I reached for my cigarettes. When I began to take a cigarette out of the package, all of a sudden the thought came to me that I did not need to smoke anymore. I had just bought the pack of cigarettes, and as I held it in my hand, I looked at it, and I began to speak to Jesus. I told Him that He had taken greater things than this from my life, and I knew that He could take the urge to want to smoke away from my being. I ended up crushing the full pack of cigarettes, getting up, and walking to the kitchen to throw it away. What an awesome feeling came over me when I did that. I knew that I would never smoke again. To this day, I have had absolutely no urge or desire to smoke. I thank Jesus for that.

I had an even more tremendous reason to rejoice that Christmas. I was moving forward just like He had promised me.

Many walls, barriers, and weapons had been destroyed in less than a year and a half, and I was excited about where Jesus was taking me. Though I could not fully explain it then, I definitely liked the feeling that I had. I was excited for the new year.

The new year came in and just as I was accustomed to doing, I went to a meeting, and as always, I gave glory to Jesus for what He had done for me, and then something happened that was like a punch in the chest, knocking the wind out of me. The meeting had been going on for only a few minutes when I noticed my sponsor motioning for me to go into the other room. I thought it was a little odd, for he very rarely attended this particular meeting. However, I thought nothing of it and joined him in the other room. He began to tell me that I would have to stop using the name of Jesus Christ in the meetings because it was offending other people who were in attendance. For a few seconds, I was stunned, unable to respond to what I had just heard. All I could think was, *here is the person I call a sponsor, and I can hardly believe what he's just told me.*

It did not take me long to regroup, though, and I responded almost immediately. I politely told him that Jesus Christ had been the One who had set me free, and that I could not honor his request. My sponsor then politely told me to just watch what I said. Leaving that meeting immediately after the conversation, I thought back to what I had been told that day when Christ came into my heart. He had told me that not everyone would believe me, but that it did not make any difference.

Today as I look back, I am so thankful for that conversation with my then sponsor. Little did either of us know that the words he conveyed to me were to be the beginning of the next phase of my preparation for what Christ had already put into motion. I had experienced a tremendous change from the person I had been. I was amazed at the fact that I had not lost control, the way I used to, whenever someone confronted me. I used to hate being told anything, but here I was walking out of this meeting, asking Jesus to forgive him, for he didn't know what he was saying. I have to admit that I felt hurt and kind of let down, but it was okay. I was going to live through it. Besides, Jesus had already warned me that these things would happen.

I was being given a new direction as I headed into this brand new year, Nineteen Hundred and Ninety Four. I knew within my innermost being that Jesus was going to begin opening new doors for me to go through. Little did I know that changes were already becoming evident in my person.

I continued going to meetings for about two more weeks until I made a decision that I could no longer attend these meetings. Though it hurt me to leave, I knew that there would be no way that I would stop giving Jesus the glory for what He had done for me. He had given me a new way and made me into a new person, a new creation. I knew it without a shadow of a doubt. The others at the meetings did not.

Nevertheless, it was sad. It was sad because I had developed a closeness with most of those who attended the meetings. They were just like me. I was there when someone new came through the door. I was there when someone just needed to talk, but I knew that it was time to move on. It was time to go forth and proclaim the Good News of the Lord to the world. It was time to go and share what the Lord had done for me! I would always have the opportunity to come back and visit the meetings.

My life had taken a unique turn. My work had now been directed to another form of imprisonment. This imprisonment was not much different from the inner imprisonment I had known in my earlier life. This was an imprisonment created by man to keep evil away. Those who had done something wrong were placed in an institution that was away from the public in order to keep them from continuing to do evil to others, in hopes of changing them into better citizens.

Though I was just beginning to have a greater understanding of what I had gone through in the past two years, I was excited because I was entering into an area in which people were being held in bondage in much the same way I had been within my innermost being. It was becoming very clear to me that, in both cases, the real enemy was one and the same. He was the same to those who were being incarcerated as he was to those who were doing the incarcerating. One by one, good or bad, we were all being led to destroy one another without knowing it. Destruction was beginning to take its victims, not only physically, but spiritually. It is becoming even worse today. Little by little, darkness is overtaking humanity. The real enemy is going unopposed, allowing chaos and confusion to take their toll.

As more and more is being revealed to me through God's Word, it has become clear just how oppressed His people have been, many not even realizing it. What a lesson on imprisonment of soul and body this has been for me. More and more people are being destroyed every single day. The battle is now on, and it is becoming more intense.

A few days after I stopped attending meetings, I was on my way to the store when I heard the words within me, *turn here*. Almost immediately after doing so, I was told to stop, and so I pulled over and parked. As I sat in my car waiting to see what I was to do, my eyes were directed to the building to my right, and I was led to go in. Once inside, I realized the building was a church. I really did not know what I was going to do, but all of a sudden, a woman appeared and asked if she could help me. I told her that I really did not know. After she told me that she was the pastor's wife, I began to share with her what had just happened, how I had been led to the building and had been instructed to go in.

She began to tell me that the pastor was out of town and would not return until later in the day, but that she knew that he would be sorry that he had missed me. I assured her that I would be back the next day, for there must be a reason I had been led there.

Before leaving, I had asked her for the pastor's name and she told me that it was Pete Valdéz, Jr. This caused me to stop, for I had known someone with that name before. However, the one I knew was not a pastor. The pastor's wife began to share with me how Pete had been called to Christ almost fifteen years before, and how he had eventually become a minister. She directed me to a photograph that they had enlarged to put on the wall so people could see what Christ had delivered Pete from, and how He had changed him.

Needless to say, the person I was looking at was the same person whom I had known years before. He had very long hair and a very long beard and mustache, and he wore sunglasses to hide a glass eye that gave him an appearance of evil. This caused people to be afraid of him and to not want to be around him.

Yes, this was the Pete I knew. I had known him because of my brother, who used to party with him, and another brother who used to work with him in a grocery store. I really wasn't surprised though, for I knew what Jesus had done for me, and I looked very evil too. That excited me even more. Again, I assured the pastors' wife, whose name was Shirley, that I would be back again. I gave her my name and departed.

I returned the next day and was met by Pastor Shirley again. She began to apologize because Pastor Pete had stepped out for a minute. I stopped her and said that it was okay, that I would wait. While I was waiting, I returned to where the photograph was on the wall, looking at the person I had known before, wondering what changes had occurred.

Not ten minutes had gone by, and I heard a voice from behind me say "Ramón, is that really you?" As I turned, I was looking at an entirely different person than I had known. It was amazing how Christ had taken the wild, bizarre person whom I had known and made him into this well dressed, clean-cut individual I was now looking at. I did not doubt the power of Christ, for He had done the same for me. It was just so awesome to see.

He began to tell me that when Pastor Shirley had mentioned that a Ramón Saenz had stopped in to see him, that he could not believe that it was the same person he had known. However, he was not doubting it, because he knew very well the power of Jesus Christ. After going into his office, I began to tell him of the wonderful things that had happened to me over the almost year and a half since Christ had come into my life, and of how I had been directed to the church. I was so excited that I could not talk fast enough, but it all eventually came out. Before I realized it, I had been talking for over an hour, sharing the great things that had happened to me.

At that point, Pete made a statement that stopped me in my tracks. He said to me, "Do you want me to tell you why you are here?" After my agreement, he proceeded to tell me of a prison ministry the church had and how he had been praying for help in the ministry because it lacked people who understood what the prisoners were feeling, people who were not afraid.

He went on to tell me that two days before my arrival at the church he had been on his knees, praying and asking God to please send the ministry people who would know how the prisoners felt and would not be afraid. He then told me, "and, here you are!" We talked for awhile longer, and before I left he asked me to pray about what we had talked about. I told him that I would, and that I would get back with him.

I left the church and went home to get dressed for work. I had a lot to think about at work, but I had already made a decision. Was it a coincidence that I had stopped at this particular church? Maybe! But, I did not think so. I truly believe, even to this day, that Jesus had this planned all along. This was to be the beginning of what I had been called to do. This was what I had felt when I was leaving AA. This was where he had wanted me to begin, and this would be the beginning of my preparation.

As I left the church that first day, I knew that I would be returning. I was so sure that Jesus had planned this that I was determined not to be disobedient. I had already committed to serving Him in whatever He called me to do—on that very first day when He came upon me.

I returned to the church the very next morning and shared my decision with Pastor Pete. As we talked, I learned that the person who headed the prison ministry was Carlos Torres, Jr., who just happened to be one of my first cousins. Another coincidence? Possibly, but I don't think so. I recall that Carlos had invited me to attend this church about four or five years earlier, but of course I would not hear anything about God in those days. I received it as a confirmation, though, that this had been set into motion by Jesus.

It was really great starting to work with Carlos. I became involved in the ministry almost immediately. Only a matter of days had passed since attending my last AA meeting, and here I was ready to begin one-on-one visits at a local prison facility. From that point on, I knew that I was doing what Jesus had wanted me to do. Where I was heading, I did not know, but I knew that He had full control of the direction of my life. I was going to do whatever He placed in my heart to do.

Arriving at Jesus Is Lord Ministries, the church I had been led to, did not come as a total surprise to me. It only allowed me to see that Christ truly had control of my life. He had known those areas that were a heavy bondage to

His children, and He knew that only someone who had been trapped under the same conditions would know and understand the emotional roller coaster that was going on inside. Here I had been led to a church whose pastor had lived basically the same type of life that Jesus had taken me from. Coincidence? Maybe, but I don't think so!

He knew that alcohol and drugs had been part of my life, and He therefore directed me to help in those areas. He knew that prisoners needed to feel that the other person knows exactly what they are going through in order for them to listen—simply put, they need someone who can relate.

People who are struggling must also know that there really is hope, and that can only happen when one truly believes that the person attempting to reach them knows exactly how they feel and understands the obstacles facing them.

The task is not only about removing the outer appearance of the problem, but about reaching deep down into a person's innermost being and dealing with the true enemy that holds the person in bondage. Likewise, prisoners in man-made prisons must know that the person attempting to reach them knows what it feels like to have been humiliated, shamed, and placed behind bars. They need to know that the person trying to reach them knows what it feels like to go to a cell at night and to lie on the bed, wishing they had not been so dumb as to get themselves into the position they are in now.

They need to know that the person trying to reach them knows what it feels like to just lie on their bed and to have the tears start coming out, wondering where they went wrong.

They need to know that the person trying to reach them knows of the loneliness and sadness that becomes a part of them, day in and day out.

They need to know that the person trying to reach them knows of the misunderstandings of family members, and of the true sorrows that lie within their hearts for what they did and for the abuse they have put their families through.

They need to know that someone really does know what they are going through, and that they are not fake. They need to know that the person who is attempting to reach them truly does care for them, and desires only to see them become free.

All of this Jesus knew ahead of time. He knew that it would take someone whose life had been just as messed up, who had been at the bottom of the barrel, and had had no other place to turn. Someone who, because of their own bondage, would know exactly what others were feeling and would not have to pretend.

Jesus knew that a person could not talk about something they knew nothing about; that a person could not talk about alcohol if they had never drunk; that a person could not talk about drugs if they had never used; that a person could not talk about hatred if they had never hated; that a person could not talk about loneliness, or sadness, or bitterness, or even about joy, if they had never felt these emotions, and, likewise, a person could not talk about Jesus if they did not know Him.

Two years later, a little over four years after I received Christ, He gave me an entirely new direction. Though He still has me working in sharing the Gospel with those who are in man-made prisons, He now has given me an even greater challenge—helping to free those who are bound in their own inner prisons.

All around me I have seen God's children being destroyed in many different ways. New illusions are popping up at a record pace to justify or to blame: suicides, killings, murders, diseases, hatreds, anger, just to name a few. With every day that passes, it is becoming worse: fathers against sons, mothers against daughters, children against parents, friends against friends, families against families, total chaos and destruction. Not one day passes that I cannot pick up the paper and read about what I have just listed.

The time has come to put the blame where it really belongs. It is time that the real enemy is exposed. God's children (and by God's children, I mean that anyone born has His Spirit, whether they know it or not) are being destroyed for lack of knowledge. It is time that all begin understanding this if they are to have a chance to be set free. Evil must be exposed. The true culprit must be exposed for what he has been doing to God's children.

My brothers and sisters, no more does anyone have to remain bound within the ugly walls, the ugly invisible bars, and those ugly chains that have been keeping you from knowing the truth. You can and will be set free, if you choose. You do not have to end in bondage. I am giving personal testimony that we have been lied to and that the real enemy does not care what happens to you.

You are not worthless. You are not ugly. You are not evil. You are not rejected, or hated, or bad, or cruel, or unkind. These are all lies that the real enemy has been using very successfully in deceiving God's children.

You are not crazy. You are not stupid. Lies, lies, lies. You are not unloved—the greatest lie of all—for God truly loves you! It is not His desire that any of His children should perish. Just that in itself makes you pretty special. Very special!

Before getting started on this new journey, allow me to say that I truly do care for each and every one of you. I have the love of Christ for all of you. I assure you that if you just give yourself the chance, you will know a new love. You will know just who you are.

What I have shared with you so far is the truth, and no matter how much the devil (the real enemy) attempts to get you to stop reading (and I guarantee you he will try), don't! For he doesn't want you to know the things I am going to share with you. He doesn't want you to know what he has done to you. He does not want to be exposed, but I do not care. Jesus does not care what he wants. It is time for people to know.

Yes, it is time to begin exposing all the lies, all the tricks, all the illusions that he has used against us to keep us from seeing the truth. He has played us for dumb long enough. He has chased us long enough. He has kept us captive for too long. He has kept us spiritually dead with his deceitfulness long enough.

In the name of Jesus Christ, the devil will be exposed. It is time to turn the tables and to begin chasing him. God is bringing glory to His name each and every day. He is gaining victory, not only through me, but He will also be gaining victory through you. We are His vessels.

I ask that His Holy Spirit guide every word that is written, and that His words be spoken. I know that He will bring into captivity every thought that is not His, every thought that attempts to exalt itself above His name.

I thank Him even now for all those who are being set free, and for those who will be set free because of this book. I thank Him for preparing the hearts of all those who will read this book to receive the truth.

My brothers and sisters, it is time to stop running from the devil, and to begin chasing him. Chasing him not only out of our lives, but out of the lives of those who are close to us—the lives of our families, our friends, our coworkers.

Christ has made you to be the head and not the tail and has placed you above and not beneath. Allow the Rock to begin breaking into your spiritual prison.

> Come to Me, all you who labor and are heavy laden, and I will give you rest. Take my yoke upon you, and learn from Me, for I am gentle and lowly in heart, and you will find rest for your souls. For My yoke is easy and My burden is light. (Matthew 11:28-30)

◈ Today Is Your Day! ◈

~3~

THE ROAD AHEAD

Success awaits those who take the initiative to venture out to take the first step. It is the most crucial requirement of achieving any worthwhile goal that one may have in life. Without it, nothing can ever be accomplished. Regardless of what one is attempting to accomplish, there must be that beginning.

A child who is taking on the challenge of learning how to walk must undoubtedly take that first step in order to experience the victory and joy of walking. What happens next is the reward for the effort that was put forth to achieve that goal. It is the result of being willing to accept a challenge that will alter one's life—to take that first step. Without giving any thought to the outcome of having taken that first step, the child is somehow able to put another foot forward and make it two steps, and then maybe a third.

An entirely new world opens right before the child's eyes. It does not make any difference that the steps taken are very short ones and that the child only moves forward one foot; it may just as well have been a mile. The child is overwhelmed and ready to go again.

What makes the difference within the child is the realization that what had been attempted could be done. Joy and excitement are the byproducts that cause the child to want to get up and do it again. It does not make a bit of difference if the child had fallen ten times while traveling that one foot. The excitement is in the air, the giggles, the laughter growing louder, the adrenaline flowing. The child is totally charged up. The child's inner being is screaming, *Ya-hoo, let me do it again!*

How electrifying is that moment! All those in the house are caught up in it. Isaac's four-year-old sister had seen the whole thing, and she was off and running to the kitchen, jumping and hollering, "Mommy, daddy, come quick. Hurry! Isaac is walking." Now the whole family was in the living room, as even Isaac's other older sister had joined in, after hearing all the commotion. Isaac now was in his glory. He now had everyone's attention. All began to encourage him to walk. "Come on, Isaac, walk to Mommy!" "Come on, Isaac, walk to Daddy!" "You can do it, Isaac," his sisters encouraged him. Everybody was really into it now.

What nobody realized was that Isaac had already had that very special moment, when he knew way down deep in his very being that he had accomplished something. Isaac had crawled to the sofa and had been able to pull himself up, and then with one quick motion, and a deep breath, out went the foot. Yes, Isaac had felt that glorious moment when all things had been put aside, and the decision to take that first step was made, that moment when his entire being was so alive and filled with determination to succeed. The world now belonged to him. *Ya-hoo, let me do it again!*

The road ahead is very much like what Isaac expeienced in his first step, with all kinds of inner emotions flowing at once. Similar to Isaac, without our even realizing what is really happening, an entire new world is being opened to us.

What awaits those who venture out to take the challenge that Isaac took when he crawled to the sofa and pulled himself up from where he had been and, with one quick motion and a deep breath, dared to do what he had never done before? What awaits those who find the strength to go way down deep into their innermost being, to reach for whatever it takes to get them to take that first step? To get them to crawl to the sofa and to begin the process of pulling themselves up, so that they might learn to walk? To get them to pull themselves from the ruts that they might be in, unaware? To get them to overcome whatever obstacle that might confront them?

The things that await those conquerors, those victors who are able to overcome those obstacles, who dare to take the challenge presented before them, who dare to put out a foot, are exactly the rewards that Isaac received. What one receives is the wisdom and knowledge that he or she can really do it, accompanied by the joy and the excitement that come from knowing that they have truly accomplished something in their life, something that they never dreamed would be possible.

Imagine that moment when you are running down the track, ready to cross the finish line. You have just fifty yards to go, but you feel like you are going to pass out, but somehow, you reach down as far as you can into your innermost being. You pull up the strength and determination to press on even harder than you ever have before, overlooking the pains, the hurts, the nausea that you are feeling, and you cross the line! A WINNER!

It didn't matter that you weren't the first one to cross over. You finished the mile race. Only those who knew you were aware that it had been the first time that you had ever attempted to run the mile. What an accomplishment! Everyone who had known you was caught up in that very special moment, right along with you. They were excited.

But you were feeling the whole thing. You had just crossed over the line, and you knew you could do it again. You had gained the wisdom and knowledge that you could do it, and if you chose to, you could do it over, and over, and over again, as many times as you wanted to. While everyone was yelling and jumping and leaping for joy, you were experiencing what no one else could ever know. You were experiencing that very special, magical moment when you know way down deep inside, that you just did it. You had just crossed over. You had finished the race. Only you could know what you were feeling deep down inside.

This is what awaits those who are simply willing to take the challenge of crawling over to the sofa, pulling themselves up, and taking that first step. Can there be a price too high to pay for this absolutely wonderful and awesome freedom? Can there be a price too high to pay to know just who you really are? Can there be a price too high to cross over the finish line? Only one person can make that decision. It has to come from the person who is within.

Your own personal walk will be well worth the time you spend seeking that ever-elusive freedom that we all desire. Not just the basic freedoms that most are accustomed to, but the inner freedom that will create an entirely new perspective on just who we are, and what we are capable of doing.

I am able to give testimony today that what we think we are capable of doing and what we know we are capable of doing are two entirely different things. For until you really and truly know and are able to feel it down in the depths of your inner being, it will not be real.

The very weapons that were used as obstacles in my life to keep me captive within my own inner prison were literally annihilated from my existence. Today, I am doing more than I ever dreamed I would be doing. The fears that were within—the panic that caused me to run away from problems, the feelings of alarm, fright, dismay, dread, intimidation, anxiousness, and apprehension were all destroyed. Obstacles such as persecutions, putdowns, lies, hatred, anger, bitterness, sadness, loneliness, pride (several different kinds), and many, many more were all literally annihilated, destroyed, demolished.

This is the inner freedom of which I speak, the inner freedom which can carry you to new heights, new widths, new lengths, and new depths that you never dreamed possible. This freedom carries you through doors that would never have been opened without it.

It is so very exciting. If I could just place my excitement within you, you would know exactly what I am speaking about. It is just so utterly awesome. I want to run, jump, and leap all the time.

Every hour, every minute, every second that you spend seeking this absolutely wonderful inner freedom will be so valuable to you as you begin to uncover the abundance of treasures that lie within you, and which have been hidden from you all of this time. Absolutely nothing is more valuable, nor more precious, than the wisdom, knowledge, and understanding that await those who seek them, that await the uncovering of the truth of who you really are. Believe me, the enemy is not at all excited about your finding the real you.

A Lame Man Healed

> Now Peter and John went up together to the temple at the hour of prayer, the ninth hour, and a certain man lame from his mother's womb was carried whom they laid daily at the gate of the temple which is called Beautiful, to ask alms from those who entered the temple; who seeing Peter and John about to go into the temple asked for alms. (Acts 3:1-3)

> And fixing his eyes on him, with John, Peter said, "Look at us." So he gave them his attention expecting to receive something from them. Then, Peter said, "Silver and gold I do not have, but what I do have I give you, In the name of Jesus Christ of Nazareth, rise up and walk." (Acts 3:4-6)

Both Peter and John had known that there was power in the name of Jesus, for they had themselves seen the many miracles that Jesus had performed. They both knew that Jesus had died on the cross and had been resurrected. They both knew that His power and authority had been given to all of His disciples. The words that Jesus spoke rang mightily in their beings.

> Most assuredly, I say to you, he who believes in Me, the works that I do he will do also; and greater works than these he will do because I go to My Father. And whatever you ask in My name, that I will do, that the Father may be glorified in the Son. If you ask anything in my name, I will do it. (John 14:12-14)

I have got to believe that Peter and John were two pumped up guys, and could not wait to go out and do what Jesus had not only commanded them to do, but had promised them that He would do, through them.

They had to be charged up knowing that Jesus had promised them that not only would they do the works that He did, but they would do greater works, and in other scripture He even promised that He would be with them to confirm that which He had said He would do. He would make sure it got done. Just powerful!

That in itself was exciting to me, but it got more exciting as I began to understand His word even more. Jesus had said in verse 12 that "he who believes in Me, the works that I do, he will do also, and greater works than these he will do, because I go to My Father."

Jesus said, "he who believes in Me." That is the part that is just awesome, for He was even speaking of me, of anyone who believes in Him. That is what excites me so much. Just a few years ago, I could not have put anything together, but now, because of His mighty Spirit, He is bringing glory to His name. He has completely changed my life.

Peter knew as they approached the lame man that it was of great importance to get this man to give them his attention before Jesus could do anything for him. The man needed to know that he was going to receive something. The man needed to take that first step.

Therefore, Peter got his attention by giving him a stern command to "Look at us." Knowing that the lame man was now fully aware of their presence, Peter then went on to say, "Silver and gold I do not have, but what I do have, I give you. In the name of Jesus Christ of Nazareth, rise up and walk."

Peter and John knew that what they had was more valuable than any amount of silver and gold, for they knew of the power of Jesus Christ. The lame man did not know. The lame man had been born into a situation that told him that he would never be able to function as a normal person. Those around him were daily verifying this by doing those things that would keep him entrapped in the hell that he had known all of his life.

Peter knew that this man had never been given the opportunity to look above his conditions. He had been so accustomed to looking out blindly, hoping that he would be given something. Unfortunately, though, his vision had become a tunnel that through the years had forced him to believe that there would never be any daylight in his world, that there would never be a way out. His life was a testimony to what the world had told him. His life had become a continuous repetition of what his vision had come to accept.

Hopelessness! A rejected, disabled, frustrated, unloved, hopeless individual, with absolutely no vision of ever becoming more. The world had acknowledged this fact to him by keeping him in his own prison. The walls were becoming thicker. The chains were growing stronger. The darkness was becoming more intense. His prison was becoming colder and uglier with every day that passed, with every year that passed. There would soon be no more hope. Soon, he too, would wish that the nightmare would end. Darkness had completely overtaken this lame man's dream and hope for a different life. What had this man done wrong that would deprive him of ever knowing a glorious day in his life. Would he ever know something different than the life of misery and disappointment that he was so accustomed to before Peter and John came into his life?

Jesus had a plan!

Jesus had come to set him free. This man had done absolutely nothing wrong. His mother had done nothing wrong. The people had done nothing wrong. Jesus had a plan, a plan that would bring glory to His name.

Peter and John were able to see past what life had been saying to this man. They knew that the man would have to be forced to look above the situation that had literally trapped him. They knew that the man would have to be motivated to look to a higher place than where he was, and therefore they called on him to "Look at us."

The lame man had been placed on the ground, which would require him to do something that he was not accustomed to, or even felt comfortable in doing, but because of his circumstances, he reached down as deep as he could into his being to find the strength that would allow him to look past those circumstances. The lame man had been given a lifetime of bad reports, and the devil had used the very same people around him who, without knowing it, kept him bound in his prison.

What the lame man did not know though, was that Jesus was preparing to bring glory to His name because of this lame man's situation, despite what the devil had put him through, despite the lies that had been told him, despite how it seemed from outer appearances. The enemy had forgotten one thing. Jesus had come to find those who belonged to Him, and He was going to set this man free from all bondage. The devil had already been defeated.

The very act of the lame man reaching down into the depths of his inner being to find whatever it would take to get him to do what he was not accustomed to doing, was the beginning of an entirely new world for him. A new person was about to be born. A new creation was in the making, and the old was getting ready to make its exit for good. The lame man was preparing to cross over the line.

This lame man had been able to crawl to the sofa. Somehow, he managed to pull himself up, to take that crucial first step. He did something that was new to him. He took that step and believed that something good was going to happen to him. He looked past where he was, and he expected to receive.

There had been something different about these men who had called out to him. There was something about them that gave this lame man hope. There was a light in them that was drawing his attention, a light so bright that it gave him hope that he would receive something. The light had been turned on, and Jesus was preparing this man to see.

Peter, knowing that the moment had come, and that Jesus had made His Presence known to the lame man, was now ready to do what he had been called to do.

With power and authority, Peter's voice began to speak the words that were to change this man's life forever. "In the name of Jesus Christ of Nazareth, rise up and walk."

Peter was telling the lame man to rise up above the situation. To rise up from the prison where he was trapped. To rise above the lies that had been told him and were keeping him bound. To rise above the barriers that stood as giants before him. To rise above the challenges that were presenting themselves. To rise above the chains, the walls, and invisible bars that were keeping him from the light. To rise above the fears. To rise up and walk.

To prepare himself to receive the gift that was being freely given him by Jesus Christ.

It is not hard to imagine what the lame man was feeling as all of these changes were happening to him. He had been bound for so many, many years that the darkness had stolen the majority of any hope or dream that he may have had, any hope of ever seeing daylight in his life.

To him, life had played itself out. All that was left was to slowly wait for the end to come. As desperate as he was, I am certain that he found all of this hard to believe.

But, Jesus had a plan. Jesus knew that Satan would make a mistake, and would never see Him coming. His spirit would live through those who believed in His name. Yes, Jesus had a plan!

> And, he took him by the right hand and lifted him up, and immediately his feet and ankle bones received strength. So he, leaping up, stood and walked and entered the temple with them, walking, leaping and praising God. And, all the people saw him walking and praising God. Then they knew that it was he who sat begging alms at the Beautiful Gate of the temple, and they were filled with wonder and amazement at what had happened to him. (Acts 3:7-10)

Yes, Jesus had a plan for this lame man. He knew that he would need a direct touch, to jolt him from where he had been stuck for so many years, a direct touch for him to be willing to fight off all the fears and odds that would be coming against him, a direct touch to get him to believe.

Jesus had a plan!

In verse 7, it is written that Peter took the lame man by the right hand and lifted him up, and immediately his feet and ankle bones received strength.

No matter what the lame man could or would have done, the very act of Peter taking his hand and lifting him up was going to be the rock that would break through whatever the enemy had created in his life.

Every wall, every shackle, every chain, and every fear that had made itself a giant in this man's life would be utterly destroyed. The game was over. Satan would soon be paying the price. Satan had lost!

Jesus came to overcome the works of the devil, and He was going to be that Rock that would break every stronghold that held any of His children in captivity.

No more would the devil's tactics affect those who made the decision to allow Jesus to break into their prisons, who made the decision to allow Him to set them free. The power of the enemy had already been defeated. The giants had been toppled over and destroyed.

Jesus had a plan!

Having had the weight lifted from his shoulders, this man was not able to restrain himself from doing those things that are recorded for us directly following Peter's act, when he reached down and took his right hand to lift him up.

The joy and excitement that now filled the lame man's being was so overwhelming, that he began to jump for joy. It is written in verse 8 that he was walking, leaping, and praising God as he entered the temple with Peter and John. The lame man knew who had set him free.

He had entered into a world that was different from what he had ever known in his entire life. To him, it did not matter that people were watching him, and looking at him curiously. He knew that they had absolutely no idea what had just happened to him. He knew that they would never understand unless they experienced it themselves.

Yes, the lame man had taken the first step. Somehow, he had been able to reach into his innermost being to seek out the strength to look past his circumstances, and now his efforts were being rewarded.

Nothing could ever take the freedom and joy that made up his being again. He knew exactly what Jesus had done for him, and he knew that he would continue to praise Him for the remainder of his life for the gift he had just received.

It would not matter who saw him dancing, leaping, and jumping for joy, or who saw him praising God, or who said this or that about him. It just did not matter. To the lame man, all that was really important was that he was now free. Jesus had had mercy on him and had touched his life. Because of this, he was now alive. No more walls, no more chains, no more darkness, no more cold and ugly dungeons.

The cold, empty darkness had been lifted. Now there was light in his life. He had been spiritually blind, but now he could see. What he had not been able to see before was now crystal clear to him. He was able to see through the smoke screens that Satan had created to keep him from learning the truth. Now he could see!

Those around him would look at him with wonder and amazement when they realized that this person was the defeated, broken down, frustrated and rejected individual they had placed daily at the entrance of the temple as they went into the temple to pray. They realized that this was the lame man whom they had placed daily at the entrance of the temple to beg.

But no one would ever understand. No one would be able to comprehend. No one would ever be able to explain. No one would ever realize that thousands of people had walked past this man as they entered the temple to pray. No one would ever realize that of those who had passed him, no one had taken the time to reach down to help this man get out of his rut. No one who had passed him had taken the time to stop and help pull him out of the circumstances that he was in. No one who had passed him during his lifetime had taken the time to stop and help strengthen him.

All that was ever done for him was to carry him to the entrance so he could beg for alms while they went into the temple to pray. No one would ever understand! The darkness had prevailed all around this man, where no one had been able to see what was really going on until Jesus had made Himself known through Peter and John.

It did not matter though. The lame man was now free! The lame man had crossed the finish line. The lame man was a winner! It did not matter anymore.

> Therefore, submit to God. Resist the devil, and he will flee from you. (James 4:7)

◄ **Today Is Your Day!** ►

— 4 —

A New Understanding

Today, looking back over the past four years, it is so clear to me, that I had been the lame man all along and that Jesus had come to give me a direct touch that first day of July, 1992.

Jesus knew that I had been so bound that I would need a jolt in order to release me from the heavy chains, the thick walls, and the blinding darkness that were holding me captive. He knew that only His hand could pull me to freedom, and He called me from the inner depths of my being to come forth into the light.

As I grabbed His hand, I knew that I would never be afraid again. I knew that I would never again hurt the way that I had been hurting. I knew that I would never again believe the lies that had been told to keep me captive for so many years of my life.

His hand had told me to expect, and I did. He fulfilled that expectation! What an awesome gift He had given me.

At the time, I did not understand what was happening to me. I, too, had reached deep down into my inner being to seek the strength to rise up above my circumstances, and had grabbed onto His hand, and allowed Him to lift me out.

I was going to learn how to walk. Somehow, Jesus had assured me that He would lead the way. I knew that I could trust in Him, that I could believe in Him. There was something about that day that assured me that He would always be with me, that He would guide my every step, that He would lead me across the finish line!

Like the lame man, I immediately began praising God. I felt so wonderful inside, and I could not restrain myself from jumping, leaping, and praising God. I understood the hell that He had taken me out of, and the last thing I was concerned about was what people were going to think of me.

No one else knew what I had gone through. No one else knew what I was feeling inside. No one else knew of the torment, or the hurt, or the pain that I felt inside. Only Jesus. And He came to set me free.

Today though, I understand that people had been watching in wonder and amazement, practically since that first day. I can imagine the thoughts that were going through their minds, not being able to understand exactly what had happened to me.

Just what was it, that caused someone to literally make an about face? What was it that caused someone to leave the old things, and take on an entirely new life?

To be totally honest, even I did not understand for the longest time what exactly had happened to me. I just knew that I was enjoying immensely the changes Jesus had made in my being, and in my life.

For the longest time, I, too, wondered what it was that brought someone to the point, where the only way out was in the manner that Jesus had used Peter and John to reach out, take the hand, and lift the lame man out of his circumstances.

Today, I can say with all confidence, that Jesus had a plan! What a mighty plan it is. It is a plan that will set free anyone who wishes. It is a plan that will bring new life to the person who desires to take it. It is a plan that is a gift to anyone who chooses to accept it.

No person can cause this change. It can only be done through the hand of Jesus, by the Blood of Jesus! Yes, today I have a completely new understanding of what Jesus has in store for me.

At the beginning of this journey, I would never have imagined the path that He would be taking me on, the new heights to which I would be venturing, nor the new thresholds I would be crossing.

I am so grateful that Jesus has changed my attitude from "it just doesn't matter," to "it really does matter." Like everything else, I know that this is also part of His plan for me, for it really does matter that the devil is exposed for what he is doing and has done. It really does matter, that people who look in wonder and amazement at someone who has been set free from a spiritual prison within, know exactly what has happened to that person.

I am so thankful today for the gift of freedom that I have been given. I am even more thankful that Jesus is allowing me to share what He has done for me with thousands of others. I am so thankful that everyone will have the opportunity to know what can happen, and will happen, if they choose to take that first step.

I am so thankful that those who knew me before, as I used to be, and those who have come to know me since that fateful first day of July, and those who will come to know me through this book will truly know that Jesus has come to set His children free.

I am so thankful that finally everyone will know exactly why I jump—and why I leap—and why I openly praise God—and why I look at each new day with an even greater determination and anticipation to serve Jesus Christ.

I am so thankful for the intensity of the fire that Jesus has placed within me. For without Him, I know that none of this would have been possible.

It is such a great feeling to know that there will be many of you who will travel the same path that Jesus has been taking me through. Even now, I am so excited for the many new and wondrous things that will be revealed to many of you, as you too, find the courage to reach deep down into your inner beings and bring yourselves to take the hand that is being offered to you.

I have great confidence that all of this, and more, is getting ready to happen for you as He takes your hand and causes you to rise up and walk. There is such a movement I feel today, stirred by people who are desperately seeking a way out of all the chaos and strife that is overtaking their lives. Destruction is all around us, and its impact is beginning to be felt.

It is so very important that you know that what happened to me was not a dream or a vision, but an actual event that took place in my life on July 1, 1992.

Even today, I know that there are people who are still waiting for the day when I go back to where I was. They are waiting for the day when I go back to drinking and using drugs, waiting for the day when I become who I used to be. But that's okay. They just don't know. Yet!

With this book, everyone will know. Everyone will know of the hell that I had been trapped in. Everyone will know of the prison that had held me captive within myself. Everyone will know of the walls, the chains, the shackles, the darkness, that surrounded me and held me bound for so many, many years.

And, greater than any of this, now everyone will know that Jesus is truly for real! And that is what really matters today. Do you know what Jesus will do for you, if you choose to let Him?

> Therefore, if anyone is in Christ, he is a new creation; old things have passed away; behold all things have become new. (2Corinthians 5:17)

Oh yes, I have a new understanding today. Jesus has opened a fabulous door for me to go through. I have learned so many things in such a short period of time, and with each new day He teaches me even more.

What truly excites me, is that this is not just reserved for one individual. All of this is available to anyone who wishes to receive it. This is one thing that the devil did not want us to know.

I can attest to the words spoken in the above-mentioned scripture. Truly one does become a new creation. The old really does pass away, and all things really do become new.

This is exactly the reason why those who are around someone who has been set free, truly free, look in wonder and amazement. They don't understand what has happened.

But now the truth is going to be made known. People are going to know exactly what the devil has been doing. People will know that Jesus has given us authority over all the power of the enemy. Not just some of it, but over all the power of the enemy! A greater understanding will be attained, as Jesus begins to reveal more and more of His word.

There is a process that one must go through, to go from old to new, and as in all else, Jesus leads the way. That's what makes it so great. The new is a sure thing, if you will just believe.

I am simply the one that Jesus is using to give testimony that this is for real. Those that knew me before could give testimony of how I have really changed: my wife, my children, my friends, my employer, my coworkers, my mother, my brother, my sister, my aunts, my uncles, my cousins, my dad (if he were alive today), my nieces, my nephews, my in-laws (if they were alive today), my brothers-in-law, my sisters-in-law. Believe me, they total in the hundreds.

Hundreds could give testimonies stating what I used to be like. Many of these are waiting for that day to come when I fall back, not because they want me to, but because this is just something that they do not comprehend. But I believe that Jesus is even clearing that up for me, and more and more of the people from my past are beginning to believe that the change just might be for good. *Praise the Lord!*

Now along with believing, because of what their natural eyes have seen, all will know of the awesome power of Jesus Christ. They will know exactly what happened to me. No more will anyone have to look with wonder and amazement. They will know exactly why I am different.

That, to me, is the most important part of it all. Having the understanding of what Jesus is really all about is definitely worth all the silver and gold in the world. For in knowing Him, you know the One who created it all, even the silver and gold.

This is not all about me. It's about freedom. It's about true inner freedom. It's about the involuntary imprisonment that the devil has imposed on God's children. It is about the breakthrough that must come to pass if freedom is ever to be realized. It's about you becoming angry enough at the devil for what he has done to you, to want to change the way your life is, no matter what others say.

But my life is different...

How well I remember those times when I would respond with these ever so famous words, "Yes... but...!

It seems that it would always be in reference to something I felt I had no control over. "Yes, that's okay for you, but you just don't know what I'm going through."

They were always used when I was at a loss for words or to help me explain the reason for my views or my actions or my fears, or to carry me through times of trials, explanations, situations, or just plain covering up for something dumb that I had done.

Yes... but...!

What a bill of goods I had been sold. No one should have to be under such inner control. It is no wonder people are so trapped, living under such oppression, such conflict, such strife, and through it all, blaming themselves.

> The thief does not come except to steal, and to kill, and to destroy.... (John 10:10)

The enemy has done a bang up job in accomplishing this. One needs only to look around to see that this is absolutely true. Whether one chooses to believe that Satan exists or not, the truth is evident all around us. It is almost impossible to believe otherwise. He is doing all of this and more.

The truth is being stolen, marriages are being destroyed, covenants are being broken, and men, women and children are being killed. With every single day that passes it becomes worse.

"But you just don't know how my life is." "You just don't know what I've gone through." "You just don't know how my wife treats me." "You just don't know.... And on, and on, and on... and on. My job, my children, my pastor, the people in my church, the people at work, my bills, my finances, my weaknesses, my enemies... and the list continues to grow as the darkness becomes more and more intense.

The very same excuses that I used, I am hearing more and more from hundreds of others. I am hearing over and over again, from others, the same reasons I frequently used to justify my actions. The devil is really doing his job, he is using the same excuses with everyone, and he has been very successful. How stunned I was when I realized that he was playing us all with the very same weapons.

So it's about time that his game is exposed. It's about time that we begin chasing him. How totally ridiculous it is. Here he is defeated, and he is still able to keep people defeated. It doesn't make any sense, but he is definitely creating a lot of strife for thousands.

How well I remember giving all of these excuses and more, over and over. "But you just don't know...." The sad part was, that for so very, very long, I truly believed that these were the reasons for my problems, that these were the reasons I was unsuccessful.

What a trap I had fallen into.

"If only...." "If only I hadn't done that, everything would be okay." "If only I could win the lottery, then all my problems would be taken care of." "If only my wife would stop bugging me, I wouldn't be drinking." " If only the kids would straighten up, everything would be better." "If only I had a better job...." "If only my boss would stop yelling at me, it would be...." "If only this...." "If only that...."

"If only" were two of my favorite words that I used to try to cover up for myself. How sad though, that I could not see it back then. I had definitely been blinded to the truth.

"The thief does not come except to steal...." And did he ever. I had to have been blind not to have seen it.

But today I can see, and it is so very clear what the devil's plan is. I can assure you that it is not to see you become victorious, or to see you become free, or to see you find out the truth about what he has been doing to you.

The... except to steal, and to kill, and to destroy.

As I look back today, I can so clearly see that I had been in a "no win" situation for the majority of my life. How could anyone be free while contending with all of this every single day? I had continued to beat myself up for all of it. What a weight we have been deceived into carrying, along with just trying to survive.

Though there were many, many times that I recall feeling as if the whole world had turned against me, I know today that it had all been a lie. I know today that these feelings were lies intended to keep me stuck at the bottom of the pit so I would never know the truth.

The world was never against me. My family was never against me. My friends were never against me. The devil just made it look that way, just as he is doing to so many, many others.

I know that Satan had been hoping that he had taken me so far down into the dungeons of my inner prison, that there would be no way that I could ever hear about the truth.

But, Jesus had a plan! And, if you are reading this book, it is because Jesus has a plan for you too. I am so confident of His gracious plan for you, that I am literally feeling the walls come down, even as I write.

It is such a powerful feeling knowing that Jesus is within me, guiding me, illuminating me, protecting me. The day will come when you, too, will know what I am feeling right now.

Yes, my brothers and sisters, I do know what you are going through. I do know how you feel inside. For no matter what the circumstances are in our lives, the inner spiritual prisons are all the same. I do know about the fears that keep us from opening up to others because we feel that no one else cares. I know about the shame, the humiliation, the hatred, the loneliness inside, the bitterness, and all the rest of the ugly things that have kept so many trapped in the cold, dark prisons.

And, how do I know? Because I lived there in that prison for so long. I was way down deep into its captivity. Though the outside said different things, it doesn't matter. What tells the whole story is what is going on inside. This is exactly what Satan does not want you to know. How I pray that Jesus is using me to expose all of the lies that you have been told by the devil! All will be exposed—the traps, the weapons used, the deceitfulness.

The feeling we call pride is probably the most powerful weapon that Satan has devised to keep us bound. This weapon, along with so many others, must be exposed for what it truly is. I can assure you, that these weapons are not your friends.

Their purpose follows the vision of their master, and that is to steal, kill, and destroy, no matter what it takes. They enter into battle with no holds barred. Everything counts—just come out the winner. Just don't come back empty handed. Bite, kick, stab, scratch, hit below the belt, whatever! Just don't come back empty handed.

Does it make any sense for the enemy to tell you ahead of time what he is going to do to you? It would be dumb on his part, right? I assure you, he is definitely not going to forewarn you. You are his prize, and he is going to do whatever he must in order to win you. He will deceive you, lie to you. He will do whatever it takes!

This is why Satan does not want you or me, or anyone, to ever know the truth about him. When you know the truth, he knows that you will realize that he has absolutely no power whatsoever, and you will become a thorn in his side, just as he has been for us all along. He will know that you are now aware of the tricks he has been playing on you—tricks to make you keep yourself trapped within your own inner prison walls.

He knows that the longer that you are behind those walls, eventually, just as for me, the walls become thicker, the windows close, the partial light that once came in will be gone, the darkness will become even more intense, the fears will be more magnified, and you will begin to go deeper down into the pits of your own inner prison.

No, he doesn't want you to know. He doesn't want you to read this book, for he knows what the outcome will be. You will be set free. He knows that Jesus has defeated him and has come to set you free.

Our lives—yours and mine—are no different, but he will tell you that they are. He will tell you, "but you don't drink," or, "but you never used drugs," or just plain, "but you're not like him." Once again, I say he is going to lie to you. He has always lied to you, and he will continue to lie to you.

I know about the hurts that you are feeling deep inside. I know about the sufferings that you are going through. I know about the intimidations, the anxieties, the apprehensiveness, the humiliations, the loneliness, the void inside, the times when you feel a deep inner panic. These were the guards in my spiritual prison. I knew them personally. Do not be deceived anymore.

I do know why we say what we say and do what we do, when it is not what we really want to say or what we want to do. It had all been so confusing before. What was wrong with me? A lie from the devil! There was never anything wrong with me!

Oh, I know that he isn't enjoying the fact that you're finding out about all of this. All I can say is—good! I am going to tell it all, in the name of Jesus Christ.

Every single one of you is a threat to his kingdom. He is on the losing end. I am so excited to be telling you all of this, but I'm even more excited because I feel so many of you being set free already. I pray that every single person who picks up this book and reads it is set free. Freedom belongs to you. Captivity does not.

The toughest battle we will ever engage in is the one within ourselves because the enemy is not going to just roll over and disappear while you find out the truth about him.

The real enemy is hiding, lurking, and waiting to devour his prey. He has come to steal the truth away from you, to kill every hope that you may have had, and to destroy every belief that you might have.

Again, why would the enemy expose himself to you, if his plans are to harm and to destroy you? Think of it. Does it make any sense?

Even as you read this book, don't let that little voice within tell you, "Yes, this all sounds good, and it makes sense, but...." There is no but! These are all weapons to get you to keep yourself imprisoned. He doesn't have to do it himself. He just starts it off with a thought, usually disguised as a very good thought.

All I can say to you is: If those thoughts are about something exterior, then they are keeping you from seeing within yourself. Satan is a very cunning and formidable opponent until he is exposed. Allow yourself to seek out the truth.

Once the enemy's plans are exposed, the truth can be revealed. The smoke that was used to blind us begins to scatter, and we begin to see. Give yourself that chance.

If a person who is afraid of heights makes the decision to stand up against that fear and challenges it, the fear will be defeated.

Can it return? Only if the person forgets that he challenged it one time in his life already and defeated it. More than likely that particular fear may try to sneak its way back in, but the person will know that he has already defeated it. At one time it stood as a giant in his life, but now the fear must leave. It would be as David defeating Goliath!

> Submit to God, resist the devil, and he will flee from you. (James 4:7)

Our lives are not any different. Yes, we may all have different situations and circumstances, but the truth of the matter is that we all function through emotions. It is through these emotions that the devil is able to deceive us in such a great way.

If there would be but one thing that I pray you would receive from reading this book, it is that you would see the urgency of extending your hand to the lame man and to challenge him to "Rise up, and walk" in the name of Jesus Christ of Nazareth; that you would not just carry the lame man to the entrance of the temple so that he might beg, but to challenge him to rise, and to walk; to challenge him to rise above the place where he finds himself that day. While saying these words, take hold of his hand and lift him up; take his hand and strengthen him, remembering that you were also there; remembering that inside, we are all the same; remembering that we are all brothers and sisters trying to make it home; remembering that without you, they won't make it home, for they will never know the truth.

We have to remember that the enemy has been using the exact same weapons on all of us in different proportions, depending on where one is in life, but the end is all the same. It all eventually leads to total destruction. Some are destroyed more quickly than others.

We were not created to *beg*! And, in the name of Jesus Christ, we will no longer beg. Why should we, when Our Father in heaven owns it *all*!? It is time to stop teaching our brothers and sisters to beg. Again, look at the message being sent, and you will know from whom it is coming.

Do not allow yourself to be deceived again by the devil into doing something that serves only his own selfish purposes. He only desires destruction. Our Father has not created us to *beg*! I don't care what lie the devil tells me, or through whom he delivers the message. It is an out-and-out lie! No one is going to tell me differently anymore.

I take authority over you Satan, in the name of Jesus Christ. God's children are going to know the truth. They will receive His wisdom, knowledge and understanding to go forth and challenge their brothers and sisters to "Rise up, and walk."

My brothers and sisters, each of you is the most important person on earth right now. You are indeed very, very special. I want you to know that, for it is the truth.

My past life is of absolutely no importance anymore, other than to use as a testimony of what Jesus has done for me. What matters is the truth being made known to you—the truth of the devil's real plans for you.

> Silver and gold I do not have, but what I do have I give you, in the name of Jesus Christ of Nazareth, Rise up and walk.

I extend my hand to you, to help lift you up so Jesus might give your legs and ankles strength. Begin to take that first step. Rise up from where you are, and begin to walk.

> Trust in the Lord with all your heart, and lean not on your own understanding. In all your ways acknowledge Him, and He shall direct your paths. (Proverbs 3:5-6)

◆ Today Is Your Day! ◆

~5~

FIRST THINGS FIRST

As I stepped out into this new world to which I had recently been introduced, I had absolutely no idea of what had just happened to me. All I knew for sure was that something great had happened, and I liked it.

I was being confronted with the fact that my life was all of a sudden different and that the God to whom I had cried out had definitely been involved in the change. This, in itself, was something new for me.

Neither did I have any idea what was awaiting me. I did know, though, that I was ready to move forward from where I had been, and without a doubt, I was ready to learn more. I was especially ready to get to know this Jesus who had come into my life. I wanted to know this Jesus who had somehow told me not to be concerned, for He would lead the way, and that I would never feel alone again.

There was absolutely no doubt in my mind, that I was going to serve this Jesus from that day forth, to thank Him for what He had done for me. Whether I understood everything or not, I was going to serve Him.

The amazing part of all of this was that I had made my decision to follow Jesus, with no idea of what more He had in store for me in the days ahead. Just His having taken me from the hell that I had been in, was reason enough for me to want to follow Him for the rest of my life.

I had no idea of the peace that I would have in my heart, nor of the love that He had given me, nor of the joy that I have today. I didn't expect the wisdom and understanding He would be extending to me, and there was much, much more—I really had no idea.

If I could just erase all of the hurts, pains, and sufferings that so many of you are going through, I would do it without giving it a second thought, but I do not have that kind of power. Nor is there anything or anyone in this world who is capable of removing them. Nothing! No one! However, there is someone who does have the power, and that someone is Jesus Christ! He is the only one who is capable of healing us.

My life is a true testimony of the power of Jesus Christ. I had tried for my entire life to change my own circumstances, but to no avail. However, when I gave up trying and cried out to Him, even if I did not believe in Him at the time, He fulfilled my desires. That is why I have such confidence that He has ordained this book. It is for this purpose, so that He will make known to thousands, that all one must do is to allow oneself to be pinned and counted out: 1-2-3. You must get yourself out of the way, so He can begin to change you present circumstances. You must give up trying to change your own circumstances, but cry out to Him, and He will fulfill your needs. The enemy is already defeated.

We need only to stop hindering Jesus from working in our lives. He is very willing and ready, but He wants and needs us to be willing and ready, so that He might begin.

> Now it happened in the process of time that the king of Egypt died. Then, the children of Israel groaned because of the bondage, and they cried out; and their cry came up to God because of the bondage. So God heard their groaning, and God remembered His

covenant with Abraham, with Isaac, and with Jacob. And God looked upon the children of Israel, and God acknowledged them. (Exodus 2:23-25)

This is exactly what happened that glorious day of July 1, 1992. I cried out, and my cry went up to God because of my bondage, and God heard my groaning, and He remembered His covenant with Abraham, with Isaac, and with Jacob. God looked upon me, and He acknowledged me. Coincidence? I know absolutely that it was not!

My brothers and sisters, I had never even heard of this particular scripture, or let alone read it. I had absolutely no comprehension of the Bible. To me, it made absolutely no sense at all. I had read some of the Bible before, when I was in trouble or in jail, or when my life was in total shambles, but I could never understand what it said, and I know that I was not the only one who never comprehended nor really looked into the Bible, except when there was trouble.

But today, and I thank God for today, I can truly see. The more I walk in His ways and obey His statutes and commandments, the more He seems to reveal to me. I have had absolutely no classes in comprehending the Bible, and I totally believe that even if someone has had an abundance of instruction in understanding God's Word, that its meaning would still be revealed only when and to whom God had chosen to reveal it.

I truly believe that if I had attended a Bible college or received training in understanding the Bible, I would be all messed up right now, for it would not have been Jesus whom I would have received, but the views of man.

I believe that man definitely needs to begin studying the Word and should do whatever God leads him to do, but I am so thankful that Jesus came into my life, and taught me to remain focused on Him only. I am so thankful that He taught me the importance of being obedient and of walking in His statutes and commandments. I am so thankful that He taught me about deliverance—deliverance from all that man wants to hang onto. It's not easy for one to let go of what he is accustomed to, but that is what must happen if one is to be delivered.

I believe that it took my complete surrender from the person I had been, and my cry for help, to open the door for Jesus to come in. For as long as I attempted to maintain control, I would have kept the door shut. I understand today, that Jesus does not force Himself on us, but patiently waits for us to cry out to Him, and then, and only then, can He move in. He loves us so much that He just patiently waits. And waits. And waits.

He wants us to choose Him, and that is why He will never force Himself into our lives. He wants us to choose Him. When you do choose Him, get ready! What a journey He takes us on. It is such a fabulous way to live. You will ask yourself, over and over, why did I wait so long. I know—because I did.

If only I could make my excitement jump out of these pages, you would know exactly what I mean. From day one, it has been just tremendous, even with all the trials and tribulations that I have gone through.

However, just because I experienced this change in my life, the everyday trials and challenges did not stop. They are just taken care of for me, and I like that. You can bet that I am forever jumping, and leaping, and praising God.

For the majority of the first forty-six years of my life, I tried being miserable, and hateful, and bitter, and angry, and all that other ugly stuff, and I can tell you right now, that I did not like it. Oh, I'm not saying that I did not have good times during those years, but they are nothing compared to what I have had since my life took a new direction.

But again, Jesus will not force His way into your life. He wants you to choose Him. He wants you to truly want Him in your life—not just because of something that you might have heard that made you want to try Him out. He loves you so very, very much that He does not want you to do something that you do not want to do.

The way I see it, I'm certain that if I chose to, all I would have to do is to ask Him to return me to what I was before, and He would accommodate me. I know that I could have all the misery and all the torment and all the suffering that I had before, just by choosing to go back. But why would I? I am here to say to you that there is absolutely no comparison.

You can choose to stay in misery if you want, but I have tried it—been there—and do not care to have it back. Believe me, I say this with all the love that I have in my heart for you. I am not saying this to be cruel or mean. I know what it is like, and I cannot imagine anyone wanting to go back to the control and devastation of my former life, for it sure wasn't any fun at all.

Yes, I do wish I could just erase all those hurts, pains, and sufferings for you, but just to remove all of these things that are not of God without your understanding what has happened or how they came about, would simply be in vain. It is very important that you know. It would be like giving a fish to someone who is hungry so that they might eat. Very soon they would be hungry again. It would be attempting to correct the symptom without looking to correct the cause.

But if someone were to show the hungry person how to fish, they would not only feed their hunger, but would show them how to get more on their own, so they would never go hungry again.

Its kind of like reaching out your hand to the lame man and causing him to look up above his circumstances. This allows him to be strengthened to do those things that God created him to do, and to not do that which man was teaching him to do all of his life—beg!

To just to be able to remove the outward appearance, that weapon used against us, with no understanding as to why, would be utterly in vain, and this is exactly what I believe in my heart that Jesus has ordained for me to do. Though I had no one showing me what I would be facing, or what was awaiting me, I knew that Jesus would be showing me what to do, that He would prepare me for the work He had in store for me, the work I am doing today.

Since July 1, 1992, I have been taught many, many things, and I have been instructed to begin sharing this knowledge with you. It is just not enough to say to someone that all they need to do is this or that, or that if they follow this procedure or that procedure, everything will be okay. That may work for awhile, but eventually they would be hungry again, wanting more.

There is much, much more, and that is the knowledge that will be given unto you that will cause you to be forever filled. Why? Because, you will continue to desire even more. It will be like a seed planted in the ground, which sprouts forth to become what it was meant to be. The seed that is being planted within you will continue to grow, and a hunger will arise within you. You will want even more.

I assure you that the God that came to set me free is more than capable of doing the exact same for you. There is absolutely nothing that anyone has done, or can do that He cannot heal or change even right now. The God that I serve is a very caring God, and His desire is to set His children free.

My brothers and sisters, this is not about religion. Nor is this about any denomination. This is about way more than anyone could ever imagine. This is about you! This is about your life. This is about your living or dying.

> I call heaven and earth as witnesses today against you, that I have set before you life and death, blessing and cursing, therefore choose life, that both you and your descendants may live. (Deuteronomy 30:19)

We have been given the opportunity to choose. The opportunity to make a decision that would alter our lives. It is with this knowledge that I am so very grateful and humbled that Jesus has chosen to use me as a vessel to reach out to the lost. My life prior to my being set free spiritually is of very little importance. I was simply existing and waiting for my time on this earth to come to an end. How backwards I had been. I had always thought that a child was born into the world grew up, lived, got old, and then died. What a revelation it was when I found out that I had been dead the majority of my life, and that now was when I really came to life. I began to live at forty-six years of age!

I came to life when I experienced the power of Jesus in my life. It was then that I was set free from the bondages of the world that kept me incarcerated in a spiritual prison within myself. What a gold nugget of information I had received! Having had the devil exposed to me is the greatest victory I could ever have been given. For because of it, I was able to see clearly the purpose of my existence, and it surely wasn't to be in bondage! Rest assured, you will comprehend these very same things as Jesus begins to reveal the things that have been kept hidden from you for so long.

Once again, and I say this with all respect, this has nothing to do with religion or any denomination. This is strictly about you, your life, the choices you have, the authority that has been given you, and about the greatest gift a person can be given as an inheritance—Jesus Christ. This is about becoming the overcomer and the conqueror Jesus has called you to be. This is about exposing the devil for what he truly is and about exposing the lies that have kept people bound without their knowledge or consent.

This is not to create a dispute over any views, or any doctrines, nor to argue over this religion or that religion, over this denomination or that denomination. This is simply about sharing what Jesus has done for me. This is about sharing how Jesus was able to change me from the person I was into the person whom He has made me today.

It is to make known to you the battles that I was confronted with inside after that glorious day, up to the present where Jesus has brought me today. I can assure you that Satan was not very pleased with me, and he was determined to make me pay for having crossed over to the other side. I thank Jesus though, that He has taught me so much, since that first day. One very important thing was that I do not have to worry about what the devil can do, for he is already defeated. Once someone is aware of that, the devil can do absolutely nothing, if they simply believe.

> You are of God, little children, and have overcome them (the enemy), because He who is in you is greater than he who is in the world. (John 4:4)

Yes, Jesus was within me then, is still, and will forever be. Jesus is the one who is greater than he (the devil) who is in the world.

You see, my brothers and sisters, I know now exactly what happened to me, and what Jesus has done for me. Even though those around me could see that something was different, they could not explain it. All they knew was that they were seeing someone who was acting completely different from the old person they had known.

No one could explain how I, who had once been a gang member, was a professed ex-alcoholic, was an ex- drug seller and user, was abusive, lied, broke promises, was hateful, was a thief, was bitter, jealous, a blasphemer, just to name a few characteristics, could now be someone who was happy, excited, compassionate, loving, peaceful, joyous, kind, good, patient, faithful, and who praised God openly.

Just what had happened to make me start acting differently, that caused people to look with wonder and amazement? People must know.

It really does matter that they know and understand what happened and why. It isn't enough that people look in wonder and amazement anymore. The devil is stealing, killing, and destroying more than ever today. His time is running out, and he is planning to take as many down with him as he can. He is taking out more and more people with drugs daily. He is wiping out more and more people with different diseases every day. He is destroying more and more people through suicides and murders. So it is of even greater importance today that people begin to know the truth. The devil is not a bit concerned whether you live or die, as long as, in the end, you are destroyed, annihilated, demolished.

Well, I have news for him, for I will do everything that I can to expose him for what he really is, from this day forth. Whether it be through this book or through preaching the Good News all over the world. People will know. The Word of God will expose all evil. People will know those things that are causing havoc, turmoil, conflict, confusion, torment, and destruction in their lives.

God through His prophets warned us beforehand. "My people are destroyed for lack of knowledge." (Hosea 4:6) The time has come for the people to be made aware of just how Satan has been deceiving them, how he has been lying to them. It only stands to reason that Satan would not benefit from allowing you to have knowledge of exactly how he plans to destroy you, so therefore he has no other choice but to get you to believe his lies.

Obviously, our best interest is not at the top of his priority list, and it is because of this that I am driven to expose him at his work. It is something that I have to do. I have lived through so much tragedy in my life that it is time for the devil to begin to pay for all the torment that he caused in my life.

No more can people go uninformed. Satan is destroying them, and for me to not say anything after what Jesus did for me would be an out-and-out sin. I have been hurt enough, but more important, you have been hurt enough.

For, you see, I know about the enemy now, and, even though he is still out there attempting to cause havoc in my life, I know that he cannot. I have been given authority over all the power of the enemy, according to God's word.

My brothers and sisters, I grieve inside every time I see someone who is being destroyed right before my eyes. When the words being said are, "I'm doing just fine," or "Everything is great," but the face is showing torment, pain, suffering, and hurt, then I know better. I used to say the same things. It's time for people to know!

It grieves me to go into work every single day, and see the misery, the torment, and the hurt on my co-workers' faces; to see the fighting and gossiping that just gets worse every single day. What really saddens me the most is that the majority have no idea that it is all being created by the devil. They just help it along, without their even knowing. I know that this is not just a problem reserved for this place of business, for I know that it is happening all over the world.

Today, because of the Spirit of God that is within me, I have knowledge of the real enemy, and he must be exposed. Truth can be given only by God's Holy Spirit, and the truth is what I have been instructed to share. This same Holy Spirit will also give witness to those who receive His word. Believe me, you will know.

Jesus has absolutely no problem sharing Himself with you, but He is waiting to be called upon by you, and when you do call on Him, believe me, you will know!

> I am the way, the truth and the life. No one comes to
> the Father except through me. (John 14:6)

Jesus is telling us that He is the only way, that He is the truth., and only with Him can we have life. He manifests His glory through the one whose life He has changed. No one else is capable of doing this.

My life is a living testimony to His glory! His power is being manifested every single day through me. Because of the change that Jesus allowed and made in me, He is reaching people every single day through me. Wherever I go, to whomever I speak, His words are being spoken. On my job, in the churches where I preach, in the prisons where I preach, on the streets, in the schools, wherever He sends me, Jesus is reaching hundreds of people.

In my old life, I would not have even dreamed that I would be doing what I am doing today. I had spent my time persecuting people, hurting people both physically and mentally, and drinking and doing drugs. Basically, I had been living in a world with the devil.

But then, that day came when I was hurting so much, had absolutely no control of my life, and felt so ugly inside, that somehow, I called upon the name of Jesus. Like the the conversion of the Apostle Paul, there was a complete transformation in my life. I had been blind, even though I could see. I was deaf, even though I could hear. And then, Jesus spoke to me.

Rest assured, if Jesus could come after someone who was as far down as I had been, He can do the same for anyone.

Yes, Jesus spoke, and I began to see. He spoke, and I could hear. He explained, and I understood.

> I can do all things through Christ who strengthens me. (Phillippians 4:13)

And is that ever the truth! I am doing more things today than I ever would have dreamed I would do. This verse assures me that there is nothing that the enemy can do to stop me, because it is Christ who is strengthening me.

Though Jesus is the ultimate in positive thinking, I assure you that this book is not being written that you might become a positive thinker. As far as that goes, once you put on Christ and allow Him to lead the way, positive thinking is merely part of the package, a gift for you from Him, along with the authority of His power in your life.

Why? Because Jesus is within you, once you accept Him into your heart. And, He has victory over all. Greater is He who is within you than he who is in the world. Everything belongs to Jesus! No questions asked.

As mentioned before: "Therefore, if anyone puts on Christ, he is a new creation, old things have passed away, all things have become new." (2Corinthians 5:17) Amen, and Amen!

Praise Jesus, we become new!! This is really something that you will come to understand as more and more is revealed to you. This is what I am excited about for you—for the time when the impact of this particular verse takes hold of your being.

No matter what is on the outside, no matter what seems to be the problem, just remember: they are not the real culprit. The true enemy is hiding, lurking, and waiting to devour.

Once again, why would the real enemy expose himself to you if his plans are to destroy you? Does that make any sense?

Just the mere fact that the devil has got to lie in order for his plans to succeed does not say very much on his behalf. Therefore, by now, it should be quite evident to everyone, that there are absolutely no differences in the purposes of the weapons used to fulfill his plans. The weapons that are being used are simply to steal, kill, and destroy. To steal the knowledge that will expose him, to eventually kill all your dreams and hopes, and to eventually destroy you. He simply throws in confusion by creating different fake weapons disguised as circumstances, to keep us off track. Oh, he is definitely cunning.

Just today, I returned from visiting some new friends in another state, and I had the opportunity of seeing how cunning the devil really was, and just how little he cared for God's creation.

Sitting around a campfire the night before, a discussion arose about an event that had transpired earlier in the day. The topic of the event that had transpired led to a discussion that dealt with the issue of inner bondage and of its destructiveness, because of the lack of knowledge of its existence, in one's life. The person in question had not chosen to have no knowledge of its existence, but its existence was being shielded by an outer weapon, or as the world would put it an outer circumstance, to keep us from seeing the truth.

This outer weapon or circumstance was the coverup that was being used to take the focus away from what was really happening, in order to keep the person from discovering the real culprit, the real enemy, the devil at work. The person was kept from discovering the prison that was being formed within them, without their knowledge, and as time went on, and more weapons were formed and used against them, they were being taken deeper into the prison's dungeons, until there was no light at all. Eventually they would be destroyed—destroyed by fears, stress, phobias, insecurities, shame, humiliation, or other inner breakdowns, which could lead to suicide or some other form of ending ones' life. All along, those around the person would be watching this slow death, never fully understanding what was going on. When it was all over, they would make a statement like, "I just don't know what came over him (or her), that caused him (or her) to end his (or her) life."

As we sat around the campfire, and the conversation extended itself to my being able to share some of the changes that had transpired in my life, I was able to touch on the matter of how outer circumstances were being looked upon as the problems in one's life, but how they were really a coverup for more that was going on inside. I spoke of many of the things that I have written so far in this book that are being used as weapons against us, such as the different kinds of fears, pride, ego, hatred, anger, and bitterness.

And then something spectacular happened. The seventeen-year-old son of the family whom we had gone to see asked me the question, "just how do you know what someone is feeling inside?" Beginning to share with him, I spoke of the emotions that I have felt inside of me personally. I was able to describe the hurts, the pains, and the sufferings that I had gone through. I told him that it was then that others began to feel that I knew what they were feeling. I told him that it wasn't that I knew about him, or anyone else, for there was no magic in being able to do this, nor was there anything psychic about it, but that no matter what was happening on the outside, the inside was always the same. That in our inner beings, we are all feeling the same emotions, some to a greater magnitude than others, but nevertheless, the same.

As it turned out, this young man had been growing disgusted with the fake attitude of the world. He was growing disgusted with how people in the world showed fake concern toward individuals by asking general questions like, "What are your plans when you finish school?" or "What are you going to do now?" These were very innocent questions, and I do agree that they are asked many times just for conversation, but here was a young man who, through no fault of his own, was having his life manipulated to focus on an exterior problem. Little by little, it was creating a giant within his inner being that would soon serve as a wall in his life, to draw him further and further away from even being able to see the love of his family. For as far as he could see, everyone was guilty of having no true concern about his life, and he knew that they were just asking to make conversation and not because they really cared or were concerned about him. Or, so he believed.

I had even been one of those who had crossed his life and earlier in the day had asked the same dumb question about what he was planning to do. What he did not know at the time was that I really was concerned about where he was headed in life. I had asked because I did not know him before that moment, and of course I asked the "dumb question." I say this in humor, for all was cleared up later that evening.

As I listened to his words ever so closely, I could feel the entrapments that were beginning to encircle this young man's life. I could see just how bound this young man was becoming within himself, without his even knowing. How bitter he was becoming within, without his knowledge. How quickly this wall was thickening. How quickly this young man was being drawn behind the power of the wall and was being held captive, and it was all because the weapon that the devil was using, was being disguised as disgust with people being fake. Yes, I could see the devil's hand working ever so swiftly. I was well aware of the fact that the devil was the one who did not care. That was his job. He was just using people to fulfill his plans, without their knowledge, just as he was using people to keep this young man focused on how fake people were.

Oh, it is so true that many, many people fall into this category. I will be the first to admit that I probably was the worst one. But now, because of being set free from all this bondage, I am now able to see the truth. I know that we were being used all along. I know that we are unaware as to how we were being used to fulfill the enemy's plans, and that makes me angry enough to want to expose the devil for what he is doing. Here was a young man who was a member of a fine family, and who was very intelligent, and the devil was already beginning his plan of destruction for his life. I was angry!

Yes, I was angry because of what the devil was attempting to do. As it turned out, comments were even directed to the father by this son, saying that the father did not care, that he even showed fake concerns. That is exactly what Satan's plan is. He creates confusion and division among us to the point that we are running all alone, and then he throws all his weapons at one time to make the kill, when we are the most vulnerable.

Yes, I was angry. Oh, I was definitely angry at the devil for what he was doing., and even though I did not completely share all of the things Jesus had done for me, I was able to share the name of Jesus. I know that He will cause that seed to grow. Just like with the lame man who had been sidetracked in his life by the enemy, "In the name of Jesus Christ of Nazareth, rise up and walk."

Before going into their home for the night, I had the opportunity to say a few words to this young man alone as I passed by him on my way to the house. I was able to tell him that he had no problems that he could not overcome.

Today, I believe that Jesus had this weekend planned. He had planned the reason for the visit, the campfire, the events, and the conversation. Jesus had a plan!!! What the devil had planned for his selfish purposes of destruction, Jesus was able to turn around and bring glory to His name. Amen, and amen!

First things first. I believe that you have an understanding of what it requires—to take that first step, with blind faith, knowing that Jesus will bring to pass those things He has promised you. You need to be open to receive the words He will speak to you. Be open to trust in Him and to know that He will be with you. Take the chance to completely surrender to Him. Take the chance to do something different, something you are not accustomed to. Take the chance to open the door and allow Him to come into your life. Take the step to look up and to know that you are going to receive.

My brothers and sisters, just as I gave my new friend a hug before leaving to return home and told him "I love you," I say the same to you. I thank Jesus for your decision to continue, to want to learn more. I assure you that you will. The seed that has been planted within you will surely begin to grow. As it is for me, so it shall be with you in time. It does not matter what people say, for you will be set free!

Peace I leave with you. My peace I give to you; not as the world gives do I give to you. Let not you heart be troubled, neither let it be afraid. (John 14:27)

◄ Today Is Your Day! ►

~6~

THE PLAN: KNOW THAT THERE IS ONE!

A s I look back over the recent years in my life, I really do not recall ever wondering if there had been a plan that was set in stone for me to follow. My life had been such a disaster that I was ready to try anything that would make me feel better about myself.

Today, I see many walls being erected and put into place as I look at people and listen to what they say. The urgency to begin to break down those walls is of the utmost importance if these people are to even have a chance of surviving. The giants who have been standing guard and holding these people captive, without their knowledge, must be toppled and destroyed.

My main concern is that people begin to focus on these inner giants who hold them captive within themselves, and not on the outward circumstances which the devil uses as weapons to keep them from seeing the truth. Because of this, I see that it is important for people to not only have knowledge, but to also believe that there truly is a plan for their life, a plan that has been there all along. It is only because of the devil's unending efforts to keep this a secret that they have not been able to see it.

Jesus definitely had a plan! And with every day that passes, I believe that more and more people are beginning to seek it. As I look around me, I can clearly see that more and more people are beginning to reach out for that hand that will pull them out of their situations. There is a desperation today for something meaningful in their lives. There is more fear. There is more dread. There is more anxiousness, and there is apprehensiveness. People are reaching out for anything that will give them peace and that will stop the chaos they are experiencing.

All of a sudden, people do not care what is said about them when others know that they are turning to Jesus. They are just hurting too much. Their lives are too chaotic today for them to want to continue as they are.

This book is not just for those whose lives are at the point where mine had been. This book is also for those who lives are *not* in total chaos, whose lives are *not* filled with confusion and torment, whose lives are *not* out of hand. Yet!!!! For you see, I, too, was there once. I, too, thought I had my life in order. Everything looked good, real good! But those were the traps. Those were the weapons that were going to be used to bring me down, that would eventually take me to the depths of hell within myself.

I have heard so many, many times, "Oh, you were just weak. If you would have just been stronger, everything would have been okay!" My dear brothers and sisters, you can believe that if you want, but I am here to tell you that it is absolutely not true. It is an out-and-out lie. It is one of the major weapons that causes one to go even further down into the pits of hell.

For what happens next? People begin to really beat themselves up. They begin to feel unworthy. They begin to become isolated, deeper, and deeper, and deeper within themselves. All along, the ones who said these words to them had no idea what was going to happen next. They had no idea that those very words were going to drag that person even deeper into that person's inner prison. They had no way of knowing or understanding exactly what they were doing to that person.

Often these are family members or close friends who feel they are truly doing something good for their relative or friend. They feel that they are doing the right thing, but pretty soon the person begins to turn on himself. He begins to allow the remarks to penetrate, and now the remarks become personal remarks. The blame has now, all of a sudden, shifted:

"I guess I really am a weak person inside."
"I guess I really am not a strong person."
"I guess I really am crazy."
"I guess I really do need help."
"What did I do wrong, that the kids turned out the way they did?"

Everything has become their own fault in their eyes.

Eventually, with all these exterior problems having presented themselves, new ones begin to branch off. Now maybe the person has suffered a mild heart attack because of the weight of these original problems that overcame him; maybe he lost total control and blew up at everyone around him and was admitted to a stress unit to be evaluated; or maybe he started drinking heavily because he could not stand thinking about how really bad he was, and now people are starting to call him an alcoholic. Maybe he became so violent he had to be admitted to a psychiatric hospital for evaluation, to see what caused him to go off. Or maybe this..., or maybe that...!

The weapons are getting even more powerful!

You know, the real irony of it is that in all the verbal abuse, whether it is from someone else, or whether it is self-directed, it is all really directed towards the inner person, but no one is able to see that.

Before all the pain, hurt, suffering, confusion, and torment, it was the outer person's circumstances that were at fault, but once a person begins to shift the blame, it comes to be all about the inner person. How weak one is, how crazy one is, how one really needs help, and on, and on, and on. It really was all about the inner person all along, but no one could see.

No one could see that it was the inner prison that was being fortified with even thicker walls and was becoming darker and darker with every day that passed. It led him to the point of destruction, and continued to drag him deeper and deeper into its dungeons, while the whole time, everyone was focusing on the outward circumstances. No one could see. No one could understand. Not even the person himself. Unless there is a transformation in our lives where the truth is exposed and the real enemy is destroyed, the end will come with the person who is suffering never having been released from his inner spiritual prison that the enemy created just for him.

To make matters worse, if the end does come without the truth being made known, those who knew that person will never know exactly what happened, and because they will never know what happened in that person's life, they will never know the truth about themselves, either, thus establishing a vicious, tragic, destructive, and life-ending cycle.

The lies. The lies. The lies! They must be exposed. People must know that it is not them. People must know there is a way out. It is not like what we have been told. Oh, I hear it all the time. "Things will get better." Or, "Tomorrow will be a brighter day." Well, these statements are very, very true. Things will get better, and tomorrow will be a brighter day, if you know what your enemy is up to. The enemy is hiding, lurking and waiting to devour his prey.

For as long as people keep on doing the things that they have been doing, and saying the things that they have been saying, things will always be the same. If a change is to occur, then there has to be a change in what they do. Just like the lame man, as long as they continue to do the same thing over and over every single day, they will continue to be the same. Only when they rise above their situation by doing something different, by doing something that they were not accustomed to doing, by doing something that is out of the ordinary for them, can there be a change in their life. When they realize that they are not made to beg, that they are not made to stay in a trap, or in a rut, that they are not made to never look up, that they are not made to go through life in torment and confusion, then things will change for them. Then, they will begin to rise up to overcome the challenges.

People have to get off the familiar path; they have got to know the truth, or the cycle will continue. Someone has to expose the truth before it is too late. Wherever I go to speak, whether in the churches, or in the prisons, or on the streets, I tell people to just look around. Look around at the confusion, the strife, the torment on people's faces, the hurts, the sufferings, the killings, the suicides, the diseases, the fears. I say to them, it is all real. I do not actually have to say anything. All they need to do is to take a look around. It is not a game, and it is getting even worse.

This is the real end. You either know, or you don't know. You either become free by getting off the train that keeps going around, and around, and around in the wilderness of life, or you continue to ride it to its end, chained and imprisoned in your own spiritual prison. You either know, or you do not know!

The train looks like it is speeding up, and you can't get off, but even that is a lie. It is an illusion. You can still get off. I know, because I was still able to get off before it came to its end. Jesus had slowed it down for me. Jesus had given me His hand to help me get off, and He is doing the same for anyone who calls on Him for help.

Yes, this book is written for everyone, no matter where you are in this vicious cycle. Maybe there are no problems that are evident to you, nothing that tells you there is anything wrong, but I assure you, everyone needs to begin looking deep inside before it is too late. Everyone!

The weapons are not all disguised as something bad. They are even disguised as good. We need to look at the motives behind what we hold as good, the reasons why we do the things that we do. For example, if someone were to say that he is a very good person, that he is kind, loving, and truly cares for mankind because maybe he gives to the poor and does many other great things, helping them whenever he can, most would agree that he was good. However, if this person's motives are based on the desire for those he serves to look up to him, to praise him openly for his kindness and goodness, then he is in for a fall somewhere in the future.

Why? Because eventually, other weapons will be formed because of these acts, such as a number of different kinds of pride, self-glorification, blown-up ego, and many others. Why? Because this was what the devil would see as the way to begin to bring the person to destruction and annihilation. The poor guy would never see it coming, and it all would have all begun with good motives.

You have to understand that the devil does not care what he has to do in order to get us to fall. He doesn't care if he has to make it look pretty or not, successful, or unsuccessful. To him, it is all a lie anyway. All he wants is the victory.

We see it every day in the papers. We hear it every day in the news. Destruction is wiping out those who are unsuccessful, but also those who are successful. Destruction is wiping out the poor, just as it is wiping out the rich. Destruction is wiping out the uneducated, just as it is wiping out the educated.

It doesn't matter who you are. It doesn't matter where you come from. It doesn't matter what status quo you have. It doesn't matter if you live in a palace or live under a bridge. It doesn't matter if you're the president of a company or the lowest-paid employee. No one escapes. It just doesn't matter.

It doesn't matter if one believes or doesn't believe. It doesn't matter if you're this religion or that religion. It doesn't matter if you're this denomination or that denomination. It doesn't matter if you're this color or that color. It doesn't matter if you are young or if you are old. It just doesn't make any difference.

Satan is out to steal and to kill and to destroy. His greatest weapon is getting people to believe his lies. He doesn't care what he has to do in order to get you to believe what he creates in your mind. For the mind is the devil's playground. It is here that he wreaks havoc in a person's life. As long as you do not focus your attention on his works, nothing matters to him. However, he cannot stand to be exposed.

Even if the truth is staring you in the eye, the enemy will make every effort to get you to believe that it is a lie. One very important truth is that Jesus has come to set His children free, that it is not His desire to see any of His children perish, and that His people are being destroyed for lack of knowledge, but ask someone if they believe that. You will hear all different kinds of responses from them. Ask someone why they feel they are tormented, or confused, and they will place the blame on something that is happening in the world today. More than likely, they will blame themselves.

Satan could care less if he loses one here and there to Christ, but what he can't stand is to have that person become a thorn in his side. When that person tells others to just look around, to just look at their own lives, to just open their own hearts, then Satan starts to worry. For you see, you do not have to believe me. Wherever I go, I challenge everyone to check it out for themselves and believe it themselves because they have seen it; believe it themselves because they have experienced it; believe it themselves because they have heard it. I tell them to check out their own family and friends to see if what I share with them is true or not.

I do not have to prove anything. I have lived it myself. I have seen the torment, the confusion, and the destruction all the way to the end. I have seen the train come to the end with the murder of my father, the suicide of a brother, the broken marriage covenants of family members, the abuse of spouses and of children. I have seen it all.

There was a purpose for Jesus pulling me off the train heading for total destruction, all the way to the end. I had been falling, and falling, and falling into that endless pit, where my inner being was being held captive, to wait for the end. But, Jesus had a plan!

My dear brothers and sisters, please look around you. Please look at where you are. Please look at your life, at the ups, and the downs. Please understand that your life is very, very precious. Please understand that the enemy does not care one bit for you. If you will just allow yourself to open up your heart, I know that you will understand what I am trying to say to you. Don't allow yourself to be misled. Think about it. I do not even know you, but it is so important to me that you find out the truth before it is too late. Remember, the enemy is the one who withholds things from you, to keep you off guard. It just would not be to his benefit to inform you of his plans.

Spiritual blindness is not reserved for a specific type of person. It just doesn't matter. Satan will use whatever works, will throw you whatever lie trips your trigger—just as long as he wins in the end; just as long as you are destroyed. This book is definitely written for everyone. Everyone needs to know. The enemy must be exposed, whether we see his work in our life or not. Everyone needs to know that Jesus does have a plan. Whether a person chooses life or chooses death, whether a person chooses to get off the train or stay on the train the choice remains. Everyone must know the truth. Everyone must know about the enemy. Everyone must know about the weapons that are being used in their lives.

Only when one knows both sides of the story, can one truly make an intelligent decision. For so many years of my life, the intelligence that I thought I had kept me from hearing both sides of the story. Because of this, I was trapped in my own inner prison where the walls became thicker and thicker and the darkness became even more intense as I began sinking lower and lower into its depths.

My own intelligence of which I thought so highly, almost brought me to my end. Money, intelligence, success, all eventually bring on other forms of weapons that turn into giants in one's life—giants that lead him into captivity. Yes, everyone needs to know. Everyone needs to know that Jesus had a plan!

> If we say we have no sin, we deceive ourselves, and
> the truth is not in us. (1John 1:8)

Yes, Jesus had a plan. And, as this scripture makes it perfectly clear, it is important that we arrive at the point where we must acknowledge that there is sin within us. To deny its existence, scripture says, is to deceive ourselves, and the truth is not in us. We would therefore keep Jesus from opening the door to freedom. The only one who would benefit from our self-deception is Satan himself, which is why, even at this point, weapons are formed to be used against us, to keep us from admitting that we do anything wrong, and we are therefore never able to speak the truth.

> If we confess our sins, He is faithful and just to forgive
> us our sins and to cleanse us from all unrighteousness.
> (1John 1:9)

It is no wonder that the devil is so adamant about keeping us from knowing the truth. I mean, this scripture tells us we are cleansed from all unrighteousness. All! We receive this cleansing by simply confessing our sins and acknowledging them. It goes on to say that He is faithful and just to forgive us. Now, why would Satan want to keep that from us?

"You mean, Ramón, that the Bible tells me that if I simply confess my sins, that Jesus is faithful and just to forgive all my sins. I mean, I did some really bad things. You just don't know the things that I have done. You mean He will forgive them all? And, He will even cleanse me from all unrighteousness!?" You bet! That's exactly what I mean. Jesus really does have a plan, and the devil really doesn't want you to know about it. That's okay, though, for today you know.

I'm at the point in my walk with Jesus where I really do not care what the devil does not want us to know. As far as I am concerned, he never cared for any of us, so why should I all of a sudden start caring whether he wants us to know the truth about him or not. It's time to turn the tables on him, which is exactly what I intend to do, in Jesus' name. Amen! This work is not just about saying that I believe in God. It's way more than that.

> This is the message which we have heard from Him and declare to you, that God is light and in Him is no darkness at all. If we say that we have fellowship with Him, and walk in darkness, we lie and do not practice the truth. But if we walk in the light as He is in the light, we have fellowship with one another, and the blood of Jesus Christ His Son cleanses us from all sin. (1John 1:5-7)

The light and the darkness are two very real and distinct things, totally opposite from each other, with two extremely different identities. To humanity, light and darkness are usually identified with day and night, the light associated with the daytime hours, and the darkness associated with the nighttime hours. In the spiritual realm, however, light and darkness are two distinct forces. In the scripture mentioned, the Bible tells us that "God is light, and in Him there is no darkness." No darkness at all.

So why is it that the devil would want to keep his works a secret from us by deceiving us with lies, if it wasn't because he wanted to lead us astray from ever knowing that our lives are not meant to be lived in darkness, but in the light? Why is it that the very lies we are led to believe all pertain to the outward circumstances in our lives, if it wasn't to keep us from ever recognizing the darkness that we are trapped in within our inner beings?

Because I was pulled out of the darkness in which I had been held captive for so very long, I am able to describe those things that were a part of my life within, and I can attest to the fact that they were all surrounded with darkness.

In the darkness there was a tremendous amount of fear. The fear took many different forms. At times, it was panic, which caused me to run away from everything, so that I would not have to deal with it. At times, there were feelings of dread. There were anxieties and apprehensions. Many, many times I was oppressed to the point that I felt I just wanted to blow up.

In the darkness, there was a cold, cold sense of loneliness. It was as if I were up against a wall, and an extremely heavy weight would come down upon me and would not allow me to move.

In the darkness, I could feel the intensity of my helplessness as I tried to move around in its vastness. My arms and hands would go before me trying to touch something, but never feeling anything.

In the darkness, there was a void that left me feeling so very, very empty and worthless, while all along I continued to fall downward, not knowing where I was going.

In the darkness, I could scream, but no one would hear me. I was afraid. I just wanted to get out, but no one could hear me.

Then, one day someone did hear me. Someone heard me screaming! Someone heard me crying out. Thank God, Someone heard me. I felt the warmth as He overtook my being. I felt His kind hand, as He reached in breaking through the flesh, reaching into the very core of my being, deep down into the dungeon where Satan had been holding me captive. The Light had come to set me free. He spoke to me as I held onto His hand, not daring to let go. I wanted out. He heard me. He came to set me free!

This is the message that I received from Him, and that I declare to you. God truly is Light, and in Him is no darkness at all. Absolutely no darkness! He is Light!!!!

As I look back on my life before that day, I recall all of those times when I went to church aimlessly, pretending to have fellowship with Him, pretending to know Him. I even went so far as to say that I knew Him, that I truly knew Him.

What a lie I had been living! I was able to say and do all those things, and then turn right around and do the things that are done in the dark, those things which the Bible refers to as the works of the flesh, evil, darkness.

> Adultery, fornication, uncleanness, lewdness, idolatry, sorcery, hatred, contentions, jealousies, outbursts of wrath, selfish ambitions, dissension's, heresies, envy, murders, drunkenness, revelries, and the like. (Galatians 5:19-21)

I wasn't caught up in all of these vices, but in quite a few. In reality, even if I was only guilty of just one of these, it may as well have been all of them, because I would have been in darkness either way.

I could not say, "Oh, I'm doing pretty good," and then turn right around and gossip about someone. I could not go to church on Sunday, immediately go and do something wrong, and then say, "Oh, it's okay, I went to church this morning." This is how the devil controlled my life. He made it seem like it was all okay when it really was not. I had been committing something wrong. No matter what it was, I was doing something that was part of the darkness, and I had to come to grips with that fact.

God is Light, and in Him there is no darkness at all. If I said that I was in fellowship with Him, but I walked in *darkness*, then the Bible says that I was a lie, and there was *no truth* in me. It was exposed to me what the devil had been keeping from me all along. The Truth! The truth about the darkness that I had been trapped in. The truth about the lies that I had been deceived with so I would place the blame on myself. It worked every time.

Now, however, as I give all the glory to my Lord and Savior Jesus Christ, I walk in the Light, as He walks in the light, and we have fellowship with one another, and His Blood cleanses me from all my sin. My brothers and sisters, this is true freedom: to be able to walk in the fruit of His spirit, in His love, joy, peace, long suffering (patience), kindness, goodness, faithfulness, gentleness, and self control. It is absolutely wonderful. It is absolutely Light. There is no darkness at all.

Jesus does have a plan. His plan is to be able to reach you before the enemy destroys you, and He is doing this through the ones whom He has already reached, His vessels.

Having taken your first step toward that Light, having reached out to grab hold of His hand as it has penetrated through all the flesh into the core of your inner being to pull you out of your inner prison, it should be clear that as you begin your walk, that you must acknowledge your sins to Christ and to yourself.

...if we confess our sins, He is faithful and just to forgive us our sins. (1John 1:9)

But he who does the truth comes to the light, that his deeds may be clearly seen, that they have been done in God. (John 3:21)

◆ Today Is Your Day! ◆

~ 7 ~

FACING THE MUSIC

If you only knew how very, very happy I am for you! You have come such a long way, by just reaching this chapter. It takes a lot of courage to truly begin to take a serious look at yourself, especially when you are going to do something that is completely new to you, to do something you are not accustomed to doing.

And even more, it takes a lot of courage to acknowledge that things may not be just right in your life, and that you want to change. Not just the superficial things, but the hidden, inner things that maybe you have known but have never shared with anyone, or maybe you did not know, but found as you searched within yourself.

Maybe your life has been hectic and you just want to change. Maybe you already were aware of the imprisonment, but could not explain it. Maybe things are okay, but you want to know who you really are. Maybe you are just sick and tired of being sick and tired, and just don't know what to do. Whatever the reason, I am just extremely happy for you.

To you, I extend my most heartfelt congratulations and a warm embrace for having taken this most important step. Even right now, I ask my Father in heaven, to guide your every thought and step as you march your way to what He had planned for you from the beginning; that He give you wisdom, knowledge and understanding as you progress; that He place His warm and loving arms around you, as He did me, to let you know that He is with you, and will forever be with you.

Now, it is time to let the fun begin!! I truly mean this. Let the fun begin. For so long, we have been out in the wilderness, struggling, hurting, suffering. Maybe there are many who are still enjoying the fun as we know it in our world, and that's good. However, I speak of an even greater fun in your life. It is the joy of an entirely new world opening up to you, the joy of being taken to heights that you have never known before, the joy of being taken across thresholds you would never have dreamed possible, the joy of experiencing a new you. Even if there is nothing traumatic happening in your life, you are going to know a new you.

The inner freedom to which I refer is a freedom that can only come by receiving Jesus Christ into your heart and allowing Him to lead the way, because only when the enemy has been exposed and defeated can you know what inner freedom truly is, and the only one who can defeat this enemy is Jesus Christ in you. You can't, I can't, no one can. Only Jesus Christ can do it.

I cannot stress enough that what is happening to people today, because of the lies and weapons that have been used against them, is literally part of the enemy's plan to steal the truth from God's children in order to kill their dreams and hopes, leading to the ultimate destruction of the person inside. The enemy could care less about the flesh. He knows that the flesh will ultimately die and turn to dust. Therefore he makes the inner spirit his goal, and he will do whatever he has to to keep you from finding this out.

But Jesus also has a plan for you. That is exactly why He is setting His people free, so that they might begin to experience that which has been planned for them from the very beginning of time.

> Your eyes saw my substance, being yet unformed, and in Your book they all were written, the days fashioned for me, when as yet there were none of them. (Psalm 139:16)

Before we were even formed, He saw us! Before day one, all of our days were fashioned, planned. They were already written down in His book. Your days were already fashioned, your days were already planned. It is so very important for you to know this, which is why this book is being revealed unto you, for it was meant for you to be made aware of all of this. From the very beginning of time, before there was even the first day, they were written down in His book. Today was already planned. All you had to do was to show up. The victory is already yours. The enemy has already been defeated.

This is why I know that this book is already ordained. For my days have already been fashioned, planned. It was in His plans, written down in His book, for me to sit down and write, to sit down and expose, to sit down and share. Yes, it was all planned. Just like it was already planned for you to read it, whenever you read it. When that day comes to pass, it will be because it was already fashioned for you, already planned.

My brothers and sisters, I am definitely excited about where you are headed, about the journey that lies ahead of you. I know that you have to be feeling at least a little bit excited, but I can assure you that even more awaits you! Yes, let the fun begin!!!!

As I have mentioned before, this book is not about being religious, or about this religion or that religion, or this denomination or that denomination. This is about you. This is about the new you, the new inner you. I say this with all respect for all the religions and denominations in our world today. As a matter of fact, I even encourage all those who are being set free and are not members of a church to find one that will teach them more about Jesus Christ. Go to the pastor of the church, and tell him that you have recently accepted Jesus into your heart and that you desire to know more. Find a church that is totally on fire for Jesus! You may call me if you cannot locate one, and I will try to help you.

The important thing is that you begin to know who you are in Christ; that you begin to know that Jesus died on the cross so that you might live; that you begin to know that you were not meant to live in bondage.

Do not be deceived anymore. Do not allow the views and opinions of our world as we know it to keep you from experiencing this true and authentic freedom in Jesus Christ. Facing the music is something that must come to pass, but it is not what I am certain most of you are thinking it will be. Yes, it does deal with looking at yourself, but I assure you that you will make it through it okay. It is not that tough!! All it requires is that you look at yourself with open eyes.

All I ask is that you give yourself the opportunity to find yourself. I know that it will require some trust on your part, but I assure you that I have lived the life that many of you have lived. None of what I have written so far of my life is made up or exaggerated. I do know the hurts, the pains, and the sufferings that many of you may be feeling; I know bondage, and I know captivity; I know fears, and I know pride. Today though, I know freedom, peace, love, joy, patience.

Facing the music for me was really not very difficult. I was so tired of living the way that I had been living that I looked at this as an opportunity to do something different. I am so thankful today that it was so. I am so thankful that Jesus had a plan for me from the very beginning. I really had no idea where my life was heading as I stepped forward into this new world that was awaiting me after that first day of July, 1992, but I knew that it was going to be exciting because I felt excited. However, it was time for me to face the music.

Having experienced the transformation of the person I had been just one day earlier, I somehow knew that I was about to go through a major change in my life. I had absolutely no idea what that change would be, but nevertheless, I liked how I felt already. Looking back, I can clearly see the path over which Jesus has taken me in order to prepare me for this day. I have been instructed to go through this change in my mind, so that I could describe the changes that had transpired and the obstacles that I had to cross over, and the battles I had to fight, to get to where Jesus wanted me to be, so that you will be aware of these things.

I can honestly say that as I was making preparations to begin, it was very evident that Jesus had been in total control. Every step I took, every turn I made, He was leading the way. Writing this book so far has been very enjoyable, as I simply have been following His lead. There has been such a divine order in His words, that the words seem to just flow.

Do not be surprised at the simplicity of this message, for as I look back today, I cannot believe that I could not have seen it long before I did, but I do understand that my life had to be exactly what it was in order for me to be writing this book. For how else would I have known what it was to be caught up in alcohol, or what it felt like to use a needle, or what it felt like to be imprisoned or what it felt like to be afraid, or hateful, or bitter, or any of the many other bondages that I had been in. I understand today that none of these were brought about by Jesus, but I do know that the devil had formed many weapons to be used against me, and that he had been outsmarted, because Jesus had a plan that had been written for me from the very beginning, in which all of the devil's weapons were going to be allowed to be used against me so that Jesus could bring glory to His name when He brought me out of the darkness, and into His marvelous light.

The toughest music anyone will ever have to face, in my opinion, is having to look at just what they are really made of. Once that is overcome, the rest is easy. Oh, you will have the trials and tribulations of life, just as before, but you will have full comprehension of what I mean when I say that they will not be the same. You will not be the same. The change that must come to pass is the change from old to new. The old person must give way to the new person. Why? Because they are two separate and distinct individuals.

Unfortunately, this change is not easy, but there is absolutely no doubt that it can be made, for it happened to me. If one is willing to change, then it's already done. Claim it, and it is yours. Basically, all that's required is some honest soul searching, and Jesus will do the rest. Amen!

For the longest time, I found myself wondering why so many people who were already believers kept falling back, and then Jesus allowed me to see the answer. It all had to do with the change from old to new that must come to pass. Today I fully understand why He allowed me to see the answer, for He knew what He had in store for me to do, and I did not.

This is exactly why I am so very happy for you that you have made it this far in the book, for I know the strength and courage that is needed to just begin to look into one's inner being. That, in itself, is one great accomplishment. This is why I truly believe that the toughest music you will ever face is to have to face yourself, to face who you really are.

First allow me to begin by answering the question, "Why?" Why do I believe that the toughest thing to do is to face who you really are. Just what is it that makes it tough? As I look back over my life, it is evident that the person who I was then, prior to my receiving Christ, is not the same person I am now. We are two different people. If you were to ask my wife and family what their opinion of me was back then, I am certain that they would say that when I was my real self (what the world considered to be real), that I was basically a good person, and looking through my eyes then, I would probably agree with them. But even then, the person I was then, the basically good person, does not even compare to the person I am today. Why is that?

After having spent the few years diligently searching through the Word of God, attempting to know more about this awesome and powerful Jesus who had pulled me out of the hell that I was in, I was allowed to come across some very interesting information about myself, and basically about man.

There is so much that has been revealed to me through His Word that I would love to share at this time, but the most important to you right now is the beginning. It is this knowledge that will vault you into a world the human mind cannot even begin to comprehend, unless Jesus has already revealed this to you. If you have had this entirely new and exciting world opened to you, then you already have full understanding of what I am referring to, but if you believe that it is just a feeling or sensation that I am referring to, then I can assure you that this is not about getting goose bumps all over. It is far from it. This is literally about entering into an entirely different realm, which even the devil himself cannot enter.

Right now, I am so excited for you, that I feel like what I believe Jesus must have felt when He was going to meet the Samaritan woman at the well.

> That Jesus needed to go through Samaria. (Luke 4:4)

Jesus had already known that He would be meeting this woman at the well and that she was considered different. He was excited about the meeting that they were going to have, about which the Samaritan woman knew nothing. He could not wait to see the look on her face when He told her that she would never thirst again, but that the water He would give her would become a fountain of water in her springing up into everlasting life.

Yes, I feel that very same excitement that Jesus must have felt, for I am very much aware of the news that He will be opening up to you, as He prepares to break down every wall, every giant, and every obstacle that has stood in the way of your knowing Him. For it is His Word that breaks down every barrier, every stronghold, and every weapon that keeps His children imprisoned. It is His Word that gives life and allows the truth to set them free.

What is the difference between the old me and the new me? Just what is this change that must occur, and why is it the toughest music one will ever have to face? The "old me" knew all about what life had to offer and knew every little thing about it. You could have asked him, and he would have told you that it was the truth. He would have told you, "Yeah, I know." But just what did my old person know?

Looking back I can honestly say that the my old person knew absolutely nothing, and that would have been a very hard thing for him to accept about himself, but let's look at just what he knew.

As an infant Ramón had been taught those things that were of value, like getting fed and feeling loved.

As a young child he was still being taught by his parents, but now he had additional views and opinions being added by brothers and sisters, aunts, uncles, cousins, and friends.

As an older child ready to start school, he was still receiving knowledge from his parents, and family members, friends, but now new people were coming onto the scene. There were teachers who were going to instill in him their views and opinions.

A little older now, he still had all of the above, but was now beginning to hang out with the new friends he had met in school and from the neighborhood in which he lived. These friends exposed him to more views and opinions. The environment in which he found himself was also beginning to speak to him and was extending its views and opinions.

Ramón was now a man, living on his own, working in a world just like everyone else, eighteen years old and now receiving an even greater wealth of knowledge from the world, with its views and opinions on what the world was all about.

But now things were beginning to happen. Ramón was finding himself having to make decisions—decisions that required quick responses. There were arguments that had to be cleared up. There were the fights that had to be settled. There were the gossips to contend with. There was the hatred that had to be dealt with. There were racial remarks that had to be contended with, decisions to be made. When someone had punched him, he automatically swung back. His thoughts had told him that if someone swings he was supposed to swing back. He found this approach to be very invigorating, and he liked how it felt. If someone made a racial remark toward him, of course, he had to retaliate, for his thoughts had told him that he was not supposed to take these kinds of remarks because people were prejudiced, and they had to be shown, and on, and on, and on.

Yes, Ramón knew all about life. He had full control. He made his own decisions. He was his own man. Yes, of course he was. It did not matter that he had reacted to just about everything since he had been able to stand on his own. Unfortunately though, the extent of his reactions to the many different situations was dictated to him from what he had learned as he was growing up, and these reactions became a part of his thoughts.

His thoughts would instantly tell him how he should react to whatever crossed his path. If someone called him a name, he was to react aggressively. If someone turned in front of him in traffic, causing him to slam on his brakes to avoid hitting their car, he was to react with anger and probably call the person all kinds of names. If someone slapped him, he was to oblige the individual with a slap or punch back, whichever was the most appropriate.

Ramón was definitely his own man! But was he really? I know that he wanted to believe that he was. I know that he pretended that he was. But was he really? Or did he belong to the views and opinions that were instilled within his thoughts during his life? Just whose reactions did he really respond with—his own, or were they the views and opinions of those who had been teaching him about life from the time he was born?

The truth of the matter is that we look at the problems of our lives through others' eyes, through others' views and opinions. The problem is not with the things around us, or with the people around us, but with what we have between our ears. Information, views, opinions, and knowledge that we have acquired in our lifetime. Of course, all of this came from those who shared their information, views, opinions, and knowledge.

But is it really the fault of the parents, or the brothers or sisters? Is it the fault of the uncles, or the aunts, or the cousins? Maybe it is the fault of the friends that we made during our lifetime. Maybe it is the fault of the environment we came from, or the teachers we had, or maybe just the situations that came up.

I say no! I say no because all of them had to start in the very same manner as we did. They were born, they grew up, they learned different things, but with different people. Our parents, friends, teachers, and acquaintances were all taught by their parents. Were their reactions the fault of their parents, friends, families, teachers, environments? Again, I say no—the same scenario, just a generation past.

Now, was it the fault of the previous generation? Absolutely not! Now, it is two generations past. Could it have been the third, or the fourth, or maybe the fifth generation? I don't think so! And on, and on, and on, back and back and back, all the way back to the days of Adam and Eve. All the way back to the Garden of Eden, maybe it was them.

My brothers and sisters, the problem has not been, never was, nor ever will be with any of you. Nor has the problem been with any of your family, or the generations before, as far back as you choose to go. And guess what: Adam and Eve did not even know.

I hope that you are beginning to understand what it is that I am sharing with you. It is truly no one's fault, or at least, no human's fault.

> Now as Jesus passed by, He saw a man who was blind from birth. And His disciples asked Him, saying. "Rabbi, who sinned, this man or his parents, that he was born blind?" Jesus answered, "Neither this man nor his parents sinned, but that the works of God should be revealed in him." (John 9:1-3)

As with this particular scripture from the gospel of John, Jesus was continuously posed with questions as to why things happened. Jesus had known the reason why, and knew that all was according to the Divine Plan of His Father to expose the works of Satan, for by doing so people would begin to see, once their eyes were opened, and would give glory to God.

Though the people were looking at the physical blindness, Jesus spoke of the spiritual blindness, which everyone is born with until the truth is revealed in them and the works of God are made known. Until such time, we continue to walk as if blind, for we have no knowledge or understanding of the truth, and are only aware of what has been made known to us through what has been taught us.

Therefore Jesus responded that it was no one's fault, "...but that the works of God should be revealed in him." (John 9:3)

This very same scenario continues to happen even today. How many times does one ask why someone acts the way they do, or why did they do what they did? Or a countless number of other things.

Without knowing, Satan is manipulating the minds of people to question the works of God, but of course God allows it to happen for He knows that He will reveal the truth within the individual. If the person receives what is being told him, there will be a change within that person forever, and He will receive the glory from that day forth, from that particular individual. This was the case with the blind man as he stood before the Pharisees who were questioning him, trying to get him to deny that it had been Jesus, and this was the case with the change in my life.

There is so very much in this particular scripture that I could share, but for right now what I am being instructed to share with you is that there literally is no fault with man, including parents, and that our lives have already been written from the beginning of time, and that God has a definite purpose for allowing these things to happen so His works can be revealed in you.

Will everyone see what God is attempting to show them? The Bible tells us, "And the light shines in the darkness, and the darkness did not comprehend it." (John 1:5)

It is quite obvious that not everyone will accept what the Truth is saying to them. There were those walking in darkness who did not comprehend and who questioned all that Jesus did.

Again, in Jesus' words, "He who has ears to hear, let him hear!" (Matthew 11:15)

I repeat, the problem has not been, never was, nor will ever be any of you. Not your family, your friends, nor you, nor the guy in the streets, or on your job, or in your church, or in your club—no one. It is no one's fault. Again, at least, no human's fault. The "why" should be very evident. It is of major importance that you begin to see and understand why you go through the fears, pains, hurts, and sufferings in your lives.

I can assure you that you have every reason to be excited right now—go right ahead. You deserve knowing that there is absolutely nothing wrong with you. You have been lied to long enough.

Now, were there mistakes made along the way? Were there problems created? Were there lies put into play? You bet there were! We have been kept trapped in a world that has hidden the truth from each and every one of us, whether we choose to believe it or not. Yes, there were mistakes made, and yes, there were problems created, but I am here to say to you, that these mistakes and problems in our lives, were part of a plan to keep us in bondage.

Therefore, the "why" should be quite evident. There are so many, many lies. There are so many deceptions. There are walls and weapons being formed every single day to keep you from ever knowing the truth, to keep you imprisoned within your being, and they all have to be exposed and dealt with so Jesus can break through to set you free. There are giants that have to be toppled, evil that has to be overcome.

We were simply the actors and actresses being used to play out the deception in our own lives. The mistakes, the problems, the lies, the tricks are the weapons that have been used to keep us in captivity. They were the soldiers being used to battle against us. They were the guards who were holding the cell doors shut! But, no more!

It is time to come out! It is time to grab onto the hand that is being extended to you to help pull you out. It is time to let Jesus set you free. With every day that passes, I become even more angry than the day before, as I look around and see the bondage in which my brothers and sisters are being kept.

I no longer look at the exterior, but straight into the interior. I see the little child inside crying out for help. I see the little child hiding in the closets, and behind the walls that are rapidly closing in on them. I see the little child being dragged down deeper and deeper into the dungeons. I hear the child crying, and I get even angrier.

Yes, it is time to begin facing the music. It is time to let the fun begin! It is time to begin living in peace!

> For you were once darkness, but now you are light in the Lord. Walk as children of light. (Ephesians 5:8)

◆ Today Is Your Day! ◆

~8~

EXPOSING THE ENEMY

Praise God, for it is time to expose the enemy! From the beginning, since the Garden of Eden, there has been deception. If you have never had the opportunity to look in the Bible, or if you have but couldn't make heads nor tails of it, then prepare yourselves, for what you are going to see is going to be totally awesome. Not just now, but many times as you read on in the book.

> And they heard the sound of the Lord God walking in the garden in the cool of the day, and Adam and his wife hid themselves from the presence of the Lord God among the trees of the garden. Then the Lord God called to Adam and said to him, "Where are you?" (Genesis 3: 8-9)

That's right, God came looking for Adam! And He called out to Adam, even though He knew where Adam was and what he had done; He needed to put His plan into action. Yes, God had a plan, and He was preparing to set this plan into motion.

Both Adam and Eve were going to be part of a plan which God had chosen to use to expose the true enemy. But God had known that He could not let them in on His plan ahead of time, for He knew that they could be deceived. He knew how weak man really was, and that they could do nothing by themselves, even though, they wanted to think they could; therefore, He could not afford to let them in on His plan.

"Where are you?" God had asked Adam, but what did Adam do? What would anyone do if they knew that God was calling out to them? He hid behind the bushes! It was his hope that if he didn't respond, God would not see him and Eve and just might go away!

Adam knew that he had done something wrong, and he did not want God to see him naked, nor did he want God to get wind of the mistake that they had made. He thought that maybe, just maybe, he could keep this a secret and no one would ever find out.

This is not much different then what happens today. As a matter of fact, this really was my story. I have just now come to grips with it after finding out the truth, the truth about just how deceived I had really been, deceived so that I might never know who the real enemy was. God however, being the patient, caring, loving, and all-knowing God that He is, chose to hang around until Adam decided to come out.

> So he said, "I heard Your voice in the garden, and I was afraid, because I was naked, and I hid myself." And He said, "Who told you that you were naked? Have you eaten from the tree of which I commanded you that you should not eat?" (Genesis 3: 10-11)

Of course, Adam caught naked, was now busted. I mean, what else could the poor guy do? There was no way that he could even make up a story. There was hardly any way to cover up his nakedness now. Adam was busted, and I am certain that he was seriously thinking to himself, "What am I going to do now? What story can I make up? Think Adam, think!," but nothing would come to him, so he stepped forward.

> I heard Your voice in the garden, and I was afraid, because I was naked, and I hid myself.

God, of course, the champ that He is, responded with the question, "who told you that you were naked?"

I am certain that Adam was really beginning to sweat as he was hanging his head, kicking the ground with his foot, mumbling the words, "I was afraid."

The conviction Adam was feeling when God first called out to him had not only driven him to step forward, but now he was being faced with having to explain himself. "How did you know Adam?" God had asked him. Of course, Adam being the brave soul that he was, did what every red-blooded human being would do. He passed the blame on!

> Then the man said, the woman whom You gave to be with me, she gave me of the tree and I ate. (Genesis 3:12)

Does this sound familiar at all? Wow!! Maybe no one else can relate to this, but I can recall thousands of times I have been guilty of doing the exact same thing that Adam did—to my wife, my children, my family, my friends—just so I would not have to take the blame. The sad part is, I always thought I had gotten away with something.

And then God turned His attention to Eve, since she now was exposed, compliments of our dear brother Adam.

> And the Lord God said to the woman, "what is this you have done?' The woman said, 'the serpent deceived me, and I ate." (Genesis 3:13)

The serpent made me do it!!! Now just who was this serpent that Eve spoke of? Who was it that had deceived her by a lie? Who was it who kept the Truth from her, and told her a lie so that she would go ahead and do what she was not supposed to do?

Does this sound familiar yet? Everyone blaming every one else, this person blaming that person, this nation blaming that nation, this ethnic group blaming that ethnic group, this religion blaming that religion, this denomination blaming that denomination, but no one ever taking the blame themselves.

The very same thing that happened at the Garden of Eden is happening today, and no one is seeing it. "The serpent deceived me and I ate"; ate what? Exactly what was not supposed to be eaten, what God had told them not to eat.

We are being fed and we are eating, but what is it that we are being fed? The very same thing that Adam and Eve were being fed: disobedience! Thoughts, views, opinions, and words of Satan, deceiving us to do what God has told us not to do. Why would God warn us ahead of time not to eat of this fruit? It is because of His love for you and His knowledge of what Satan desires for you.

My brothers and sisters, it is time for all of this deception to come to an end. It is time that the enemy be exposed for what he is doing to you. It is time for all of this to stop. Scripture tells us that the serpent was exposed for the snake that he is. I can assure you that it sure was not for being nice, or because he really cared for you, or because he had good things planned for your life. I just don't know why, but the word "destruction" keeps coming to mind. Satan was being exposed for the liar that he is and for the destruction he brought to pass.

Adam and Eve, of course, were in the background like little kids who were just caught eating their dessert before dinner, not knowing what to do, unaware of what Satan had planned for their lives, unaware of the deception that had just placed them in the position of doing what God had told them not to do. Boy, do I remember days like that! I thank Jesus that I do not have to go through those days anymore. I am so thankful that I am able to make a choice today. Yes, I am very much aware of the fact that I had choices that I could make even before calling on Jesus, but what choices could I really make when it was all one-sided. I only knew one way, and that was what I was allowed to know.

Today, thanks to Jesus having removed the scales from my eyes, I can see both sides. I still have a choice to make, but at least now I am able to make one after weighing out all that I know. I can make a choice between doing good and evil and know it is because of the freedom I know in my life today. I understand the difference today—discernment that was never there before.

There are those who will say that everyone knows the difference between good and evil and are therefore responsible for the decisions they have made. I would have to agree, but I would have to ask, "Compared to what?" Is it possible to be deceived into believing that something is good because it looks good? Is it possible to be deceived into doing something you really do not want to do? How much of the truth is in what one considers to be good and evil?

Eve thought it would be okay to eat of the fruit, but was it really? Was it possible that she was really deceived? Scripture tells us that she was deceived, and that there had been a serpent who had slithered his way into the Garden of Eden to do just that. Does that make it okay? Does that make Eve responsible for doing something that she thought was good, when the reality was that she had been deceived?

Most people today would say "Yes" and continue to say "Yes," simply because one is supposed to know the difference between good and evil, simply because an adult should know the difference. Again I ask, "Compared to what?" I just thank Jesus that He is so kind and merciful, and that He is the one who decides, or else I would not be where I am today! God in His Infinite Wisdom had known all along that the culprit was not Adam or Eve, but He had to allow the disobedience to happen just like it did so He could expose Satan for the snake that he is and to put His plan into motion. He caught Satan in the act and could now tell him what He had in store for him, what his future was going to be.

> Because you have done this, you are cursed more than all cattle, and more than every beast of the field; on your belly you shall go, and you shall eat dust all the days of your life. And I will put enmity between you and the woman, and between your seed and her Seed; He shall bruise your head, and you shall bruise His heel. (Genesis 3 14:15)

The serpent was to be absolutely wiped out by this Someone who was going to bruise his head while he bruised His heel. This was to be the long battle between good and evil, with God ultimately winning through Jesus Christ. God had known that

Satan had planned to destroy as many of God's children as he could, because He had kicked him out of heaven, but the devil had forgotten one thing: God had created him too! Satan was doomed from the beginning.

God had known all along that the fault for the fall of man would not be because of Adam or Eve, but He still needed to use them in order to trap Satan. The fault was no one's. The snake had slithered his way into the Garden of Eden uninvited, to begin his battle against God's people in order to get even with God for having kicked him out of heaven. Did you catch that? The fault was no one's! Not yours, not your parents', not your family members', not your friends', not your teachers', not anyone's.

My brothers and sisters, I know that this is very much against what we have been taught during our life, but I assure you, there is definitely a direction in which Jesus is leading you, and all I ask is that you continue to follow the direction in which He is taking you. All will be made clear as you press forward. We are not a defeated people like Satan would have us believe, rather we have been a deceived people. Deceived into believing a lie that continues to hold God's children in bondage.

It is so easy to believe a lie, especially when logic tells us that it makes sense in our world. Logic would tell us that a person does have the ability to make choices; therefore the person should know right from wrong, the person should know the difference between good and evil.

But, just how much of the truth does a person really know of *the* Truth? And exactly whose "truth" have they been hearing? Eve thought she was receiving the truth, but was it the truth or deception? Did the truth she received and acted on lead Adam and her into freedom, or were they tricked into bondage so they would also be cursed? Was it not this very act of disobedience that brought sin into our world? Now, if the serpent (whom God revealed was Satan) was able to deceive one of God's children in the Garden of Eden, then is it not possible that he is capable of doing the same to God's children today? I can assure you that it is not only possible, but he is doing this very same act today, and because he is still deceiving God's children today, it is a matter of life and death that you not allow him to deceive you in this matter.

I ask you to consider exactly what choices you are really capable of making. Are they really choices that are being made because you have heard both sides, or are they one-sided choices that are being made because that is all you know? Truly think about this, for it is this very thing that literally places you in jeopardy of committing a sin, simply because you have chosen to believe what you have determined to be the truth, but in reality, you have been deceived into unintentionally judging someone else.

We can only act according to what we know. There is so much more to the Truth than what we have been led to believe is the truth. Jesus has come to set His people free, not to confuse them. I assure you that the serpent has continued his journey into the lives of God's children, even into the church. but if you will only allow it, Jesus will make the truth known. It is no secret that we are born into sin, but there are underlying issues that must be exposed before you will be able to see just how much you have been deceived.

Again, this is not about religion, denominations, or doctrinal views and opinions. This is about life and death. This is about your life or death. The serpent, the snake, the devil, Satan, Lucifer—call him what you want—slithered his way into the Garden of Eden uninvited, and nothing has changed. You are just not aware of it. His aim has been to steal, kill, and destroy, because it is his way of getting back at God for having kicked him and his buddies out of heaven; or so he thought.

But God had a plan!!!! Yes, God had already planned for there to be a battle against good and evil. A plan which is going to give Him the victory—Jesus Christ!! Victory has been ours from the very beginning of time. It is no wonder that the devil has been trying so desperately to keep us deceived. All we have to do is to show up for the battle. It's God's fight, and He has already won!! You have got to see that now.

Satan did not know who this Person was going to be who would bruise his head, and Whose heel he would bruise. Therefore, Satan has continued slithering his way into the homes, the marriages, the minds, the nations, the kingdoms, and the lives of God's children, destroying everything and everyone that crossed his path, as he tried to figure out just who this Person was who

God said would defeat him, in hopes that he would possibly destroy Him before it happened. For hundreds of years, Satan had searched and searched, all to no avail—until Jesus died on the cross! Then Satan knew!

Nevertheless, his kingdom continues to grow, as he continues to steal, kill, and destroy God's people, for along the way he is deceiving thousands into believing his lies. Generation after generation, the curse continues to annihilate. People are teaching other people the ways of the world, but whose world is it? It belongs to the devil, and it will continue to be his, until Jesus returns to take back what is His. This is all part of God's plan. It is written:

> For we do not wrestle against flesh and blood, but against principalities, against powers, against rulers of the darkness of this age, against spiritual hosts of wickedness in the heavens. (Ephesians 6:12)

My brothers and sisters, the deception has been great. Generation after generation, God's children have been taught to steal from each other, and to kill and destroy one another. Spiritual blindness is literally taking over, causing people to be more easily deceived, and it is getting worse. Take a look around you; really take a good look! Wherever you look there is major poverty. People are dying of starvation. The children of today are being labeled "Generation X." Why is this? If God created all things, and He did, that means that He owns all things. Then, why is there so much destruction all around us? Can you now see the weapons Satan has been using all along?

Every time someone speaks to a child in a negative way, the words spoken are brought into existence, and they begin to make their way into the child's makeup—comments such as, "You're so stupid," or "You're so dumb," or "Why can't you be as smart as your brother (sister)," and so many more. I am certain that you are getting the message. Satan is using us to destroy each other.

Every time a person speaks to someone else in a derogatory manner, the words spoken are brought into existence, and they begin to cut like a knife to do their damage, which leads to other forms of weapons, such as hatred, anger, and bitterness.

Every time someone gossips about someone else, destruction is brought into existence, as the words begin to form other weapons such as shame, humiliation, hurt, and pain, whether the gossip is a lie or the truth about the individual. The words have been spoken and destruction begins to have its way.

Every time a person begins to see themselves above everyone else, separation and division makes its way into their lives, only to open doors for even greater weapons to join in, such as pride. Satan is deceiving God's children into destroying one another. I could go on and on, but I am certain the message is very clear as to how Satan has been increasing his kingdom by having others do his dirty work.

Even in the church, there is much deception. Satan really goes all out here, for he knows that by keeping the members of the Body of Christ deceived, confused, and fighting with each other, they will never have time to seek the truth. The outsider who is not a member of any church is invited to attend by a friend, but the outsider begins to take a look at what the members of that church are doing and decides that he does not want to be a part of it. He sees the self-righteous attitudes, the gossiping, the false lives, the same sins he or she is committing, and asks him- or herself, "Why should I become a part of a church, or even believe in a God that these people in the church are professing to know, when I can continue to do these things without becoming a member of a church, or even having to believe in God?"

I am not saying these things to tear down the church. I am being instructed to speak the truth. Satan is destroying the children of God at a more rapid pace today than ever before, and it is grieving my heart. People are hurting inside, but they have no place to turn. In their eyes, there is no hope. I was that person. I was the one who would be invited to go to different churches. These were my very thoughts after visiting those churches. Why should I have stayed? I was already doing those things I knew many in the churches were doing. I did not have to become a believer in Christ. I was already having fun, enjoying myself, getting drunk, doing drugs, partying, being lustful, greedy, hateful, bitter, envious, lying, and abusive. Why would I want to become like the person at work who went around preaching to everyone else about how they needed to change or they would go to hell, when I knew that the person was doing the same things I was doing, and then to top it off, getting slammed for doing it? No thank you, I didn't need all that.

My brothers and sisters, and I say this to all of you, whether you are a believer or not, a member of a church or not, Satan is disguising his weapons in such a way that he has us stealing the Word of God from ourselves, killing our hopes and dreams, which will ultimately lead to the end of the road—destruction! It is extremely urgent that we begin to expose Satan's works.

> Death and life are in the power of the tongue, and those who love it will eat its fruit. (Proverbs 18:21)

This is not about this church being right, or that church being wrong, nor about this denomination being right, or that denomination being wrong. This is about the weapons that are being used against you, to cause us to destroy one another, while Satan sits back and laughs. No more! This is about allowing your hearts and eyes to be open, so that you can begin to see the truth. Everything I have written so far is happening. I do not have to make it up. Again, do not believe me, but allow the Spirit of God within you to cause you to look around. You will see that all I have written so far is the truth.

Satan is using the exact same weapons over and over and over again, on everybody. Our situations and our circumstances may be different, but inside, the weapons are all the same. It's time to wake up, people. It's time to see things as they really are. It's time to clean out the house, the whole house—not just where visitors can see, but in the corners and under the rugs. It is time to see the enemy for who and what he really is, a liar, a deceiver, and an enemy of God!

You are not the enemy. Your family is not the enemy. Your friends are not the enemy. I am not the enemy. It's time to stop treating each other as if we were. It's time to stop slamming your spouse, or that brother or sister at work, or that person who does not believe, or that person who does believe, or your boss, or whomever! It is time to stop before we totally destroy each other.

There truly is death and life in the power of the tongue. What you speak will truly come to pass. What you sow, you shall reap. If that is truly the case, then why not begin speaking life instead of death into a person's life, into a so-called enemy's life— now that we understand that they truly are not the enemy.

If the statement, "you will reap what you sow" is true, and I can assure you that it is, then why not begin saying good things about each other, so that we can reap good things? Why would you sow a curse into someone's life, if you know that the same curse is coming back to you? Make sense? Do not allow the weapons formed by Satan to keep you from seeing the truth and understanding the simplicity of this statement.

Another well known phrase is "Do unto others, as you would have them do unto you." I have to believe that just about everyone who is capable of hearing has heard this statement before. Do good to receive good. Do bad to receive bad. You shall reap what you sow. There truly is death and life in the power of the tongue.

Do you see what Satan has been doing to God's people? Do you see what Satan has been doing to you? I am amazed, since finding out that Satan was defeated, at just how he is able to keep God's children in bondage, and with every generation that passes, the truth is getting further and further away from us. Satan has had less and less to do to keep us captive. His kingdom is continuing to grow, and he is growing an army to do his dirty work.

I am certain that you can see now just how he has been having us do all of those things we were not supposed to be doing, all on our own. It is getting completely out of hand. Morals and values are becoming a thing of the past, if they are not already. People are attacking each other mentally, verbally, and physically more than ever before, yet no one can see. People are buying into sin more than ever before. Absolutely nothing is sacred anymore. People are buying into sexual immorality, into wickedness, into maliciousness, into envy, into greed, into evil, more than ever before, and it is becoming worse. Hearts are being hardened, as vile passions become the accepted part of today's society. Satan is stealing the Word of God from us. Little by little, day by day, year by year, generation after generation,

God's Word is being stolen so that one will never know the truth. Satan knew that there was life in the Word of God, and he had to keep us from finding that out.

People have been reacting with the thoughts of the devil. Of course, this is because of deception, lies, weapons, strongholds. Any type of deception would get the job done, and the worse it gets, the further away from the truth people are taken. The inner person is being dragged further and further into the deepest part of the prison within.

I say this to my younger brothers and sisters who have been deceived into believing that they are a lost generation. You are not a lost generation; this is an out-and-out lie, a game piece in Satan's defeated plan to destroy, which is being exposed for the lie that it is. The truth will be made known, even if I have to go all over the world saying it.

I know that what I speak will come to pass, for Jesus has assured us that anything we ask in His name, if we do not doubt, He will do. Therefore, poverty and starvation, you are on your way out; there is no generation X, but a generation of God's children who are winners. Believe me, *I do not doubt!* Amen and amen!!

And how do I know? I know because God had a plan! The battle has begun against good and evil, and Satan will now be exposed for who and what he is—a liar! Jesus has come to set His children free!! In the Gospel of John 10:10, we see where it was written that "the thief does not come except to steal, and to kill, and to destroy..." But there is a second part to the scripture that is even more important to know, and that is: "I have come that they may have life, and that they may have it more abundantly." Thank you Jesus!!!!

Yes, God had a plan, and that plan was Jesus Christ! Jesus tells us that He has come that we may have life, and have it more abundantly. Jesus is telling us that it does not matter what the devil has done to deceive you; it is over, if you will believe. Jesus has already defeated the enemy. We need but to walk in the victory, to walk in the truth. We are definitely not a defeated people; we have only been a deceived people, and Jesus is taking care of that.

Our problems are not around us. Our problems are not even with those who are in our lives. Actually, we are all in the same boat, and we just haven't known it. Our problems are not even about us. The problem we have is in our thoughts, in how we perceive those things that are happening to us. I am already very much aware of the answers that would be given if we did not have any of the knowledge that God has revealed in His Word.

One of Satan's major weapons is confusion, and this is exactly how he keeps so much chaos and turmoil alive in our world today. He uses confusion within the church, within the homes, and within the marriage covenants. He uses confusion within the workplace, within the world, and within our minds. As long as he can keep confusion alive, there will never be any unity. If there is confusion, there will always be separation and division.

> Every kingdom divided against itself is brought to desolation, and every city or house divided against itself will not stand. (Matthew 12:25)

Jesus had warned us that this would happen, so if He knew beforehand, then He also knew that He would be there to protect you, and bring peace into your life. My brothers and sisters, confusion and fear are not of God. It is not my goal to pick on the churches. My goal is to have everyone possible to start seeing the truth, to begin knowing the truth about the enemy, to begin knowing the truth about themselves. For it is in knowing, that we are set free. Satan will not relinquish that which he has gained without a fight, but neither you nor I have got to fight, for "thus says the Lord to you: 'Do not be afraid nor dismayed because of this great multitude, for the battle is not yours, but God's.'" (2Chronicles 20:15). God has sent His Son to defeat Satan!

It would be easy to point the finger at someone else, like Adam did to Eve, and to blame them for what is happening in your lives, but when it comes to pointing the finger at oneself, then it becomes extremely difficult. No one likes to admit that they have made mistakes, let alone having to acknowledge it, but that is the beginning of stepping into freedom, and it is something that has to be done.

God is good, and He is very much aware of your situations and circumstances before they even happen, and is also very aware that you have been deceived. He knows that the wrongdoer has not been us. Just like He knew that it was not Adam or Eve. He gave them life, and they were winners, just like you and I are, but they were deceived, just like you and I have been.

Yes, we all fall short of the glory of God, but the enemy would deceive you into believing that he is not at fault, and that you are the one who makes the choices, but somewhere, sometime, we have got to come to grips with the truth. We have got to see that we are not capable of doing anything on our own. That without Jesus, we are doomed. Just like Satan is doomed.

God's Word tells us the truth. God cannot lie, and if He has told us that "if we confess our sins, He is faithful and just to forgive us our sins, and to cleanse us from all unrighteousness" (1John 1:9), then He means exactly that, regardless of whatever lie Satan is trying to get you to believe. Satan is doomed. As is also written in 1John 1:10, "If we say that we have not sinned, we make Him a liar, and His word is not in us," and He also means that!

It is essential that you remember that you are not at fault, your family is not at fault, your friends are not at fault, and that God really does know what He is doing. God understands very well that until we know the truth, we will continue to be deceived into sinning.

God also knows, though, that once you know the truth and still continue to allow Satan to deceive you, then it will be because you have not believed what He has told you. Therefore, it now becomes your fault, for you will have made a choice between good and evil, based on hearing both sides. This is why I believe that Jesus has placed such a drive and determination within my heart to go forth and share what He has done for me and to expose the work of the enemy.

All I know is that I was lost, but now I am found. I was sick, and now I am healed. I was a sinner, and I am now forgiven. I was in the dark, and now I am in the light. I was weak, and now I am strong in Jesus. I was blind, and now I am able to see. I was taken from the darkness that had held me bound for so many years of my life, taken from the place where so many of God's children are still imprisoned, and it is there that Jesus has called me to return, to begin reaching into the depths of the hell that holds them in bondage—into the spiritual prisons where they are being held captive.

Only if you have been taken from its grips can you know how cold, ugly, lonely, and dark that prison really and truly is. The nightmare is horrendous, the intensity of the darkness escapes all imagination, and no one should have to remain in its clutches. Someone has got to hear the cries of the inner child. Someone has got to go in after them. These are God's children, and they will be set free. Whether or not you are already a believer in Jesus Christ, what matters right now is that the enemy has been exposed to you.

> I am the Way, the Truth, and the Life. No one comes to the Father, except through me. (John 14:6)

The choice is yours. Jesus will not force His way into your life, but, I know that as my days were already written in His book, so are yours. Therefore, I say to you, look around you, take notice of the destruction, the chaos, the breakdown in the world, and you will see that what I have written is the truth. Let your eyes be directed to the truth. Jesus has said that the only way to go to the Father is through Him. Jesus has come to set you free!

"The thief (Satan) has not come except to steal, and to kill, and to destroy." (John 10:10) It is time to stop the deception in your lives, by allowing the truth to come forth.

It is time for the churches to turn the light on now. Those who are walking in darkness are looking for a place where the light is turned on. They cannot see, and they need the light to guide them. How can someone in darkness enter into a place that is just as dark inside as he feels? They would not be able to see it and would walk right on by. and I can assure the churches that this is happening every single day.

Trust me, I am speaking from experience. As I was being dragged further and further into the dungeons of my spiritual prison, I could hear myself crying inside, but no one could hear me. Someone has got to hear, but the light inside has to be on first. Do not allow Satan to continue to deceive you with his lies.

He does not care one bit for you, but he definitely keeps trying to deceive you. He has put too much effort into your life to just give you up without a fight, but it does not matter what he tries to do, for you already have the victory, and all you need to do is to stand still and watch the salvation of the Lord. All you need to do is to allow Jesus to pull you out, and He will do the rest.

We are at the point now where the old has got to go, and the new has got to come in. Satan would have you think differently though, but do not allow him to, now that you know exactly what and who he is. This is why the enemy had to be exposed!!!

> Then Jesus spoke to them again, saying, "I am the light of the world. He who follows Me shall not walk in darkness, but have the light of life." (John 8:12)

◄ Today Is Your Day! ►

~9~

THE PROMISED LAND

The order to cross the Jordan was given to the people of Israel by Joshua:

> Then Joshua commanded the officers of the people saying, "Pass through the camp and command the people saying, Prepare provisions for yourselves, for within three days you will cross over this Jordan, to go in to possess the land which the Lord your God is giving you to possess." (Joshua 1:10-11)

> Remember the word which Moses the servant of the Lord commanded you saying, "The Lord your God is giving you rest and is giving you this land." (Joshua 1:13)

> Then Joshua rose early in the morning; and they set out from Acacia Grove and came to the Jordan, he

and all the children of Israel, and lodged there before they crossed over. (Joshua 3:1)

So it was, after three days, that the officers went through camp; and they commanded the people, saying, 'When you see the ark of the covenant of the Lord your God, and the priests, the Levites, bearing it, then you shall set out from your place and go after it; (Joshua 3:2-3)

Yet there shall be a space between you and it, about two thousand cubits by measure. Do not come near it, that you may know the way by which you must go, for you have not passed this way before. (Joshua 3:4)

And Joshua said to the people, "Sanctify yourselves, for tomorrow the Lord will do wonders among you." (Joshua 3:5)

Then the priests who bore the ark of the covenant of the Lord stood firm on dry ground in the midst of the Jordan, and all Israel crossed over on dry ground, until all the people had crossed over completely over the Jordan. (Joshua 3:17)

They had crossed into the Promised Land, the land God had promised to give to Abraham when He told him to

Get out of your country, from your family, and from your father's house, to a land that I will show you. (Genesis 12:1)

The promised land was the land He had promised Moses,

So I have come down to deliver them out of the hand of the Egyptians, and to bring them up from the land to a good and large land, to a land flowing with milk and honey.... (Exodus 3:8)

The promised land was the land He had promised Joshua when He told him,

> Moses my servant is dead, now therefore, go over the Jordan, you and all this people, to the land which I am giving them, the children of Israel. (Joshua 1:2)

The promised land was the land in which Isaiah wrote,

> Your eyes will see the King in His beauty; they will see the land that is very far off. (Isaiah 33:17)

The promised land, the land on the other side of the Jordan; so close, but yet so far. The waters rising high on its banks, yet the land must be reached. Nevertheless, it is the land that remains so elusive to many, the land that so many are not willing to go into, the land that has been promised, but yet remains a dream to thousands of God's people. Why?

Just what is it about this land that keeps thousands upon thousands of God's people from ever crossing over this Jordan River to receive its treasures? Just what is it about this land that keeps thousands from receiving the promises that would be fulfilled, if only they would cross over, for God has given His word, and God cannot lie?

Just what is it that will continue to be a barrier that causes people to turn back from ever reaching its fullness? Just what is it that keeps thousands on the other side looking, but unwilling to make the effort to just cross over? Thousands upon thousands will find themselves in the same position as those who were told that they would not be able to cross over. Instead, they would wander in the wilderness until the end, and they would die there.

> And the Lord heard the sound of your words, and was angry, and took an oath, saying. "Surely not one of these men of this evil generation shall see that good land of which I swore to give to your fathers." (Deuteronomy 1:34-35)

And these were God's people!!

> *Oh my Father in heaven, extend your mercy and kindness upon your children, that they might begin to see the truth of what is happening. Allow these words to reach them before the lies of the devil totally wipe them out. Do not allow the deception of the enemy to continue to blind them from the truth. Father, bring your children out of this spiritual darkness, for these are your children for whom You sent Your Only Begotton Son to die on the cross, that they might have eternal life. And all because you loved us. Let your truth stir their innermost being.*

My brothers and sisters, thousands are coming to the Jordan every single minute of every single day of every single year, and thousands are being turned back by the deception of the enemy. They are turned away from that moment of truth as they look across the Jordan, in that very moment that will determine what they will do. It is the moment when they see the deep waters rising high against the banks. It is the moment when the noise of the waters splashing against the river bank causes them to have fear, as they look upon their own personal life.

They are turned away from the moment of truth when the giants in their lives begin to stand tall before them, between them and the Jordan, causing the children of God to withdraw, afraid. Because the father of lies is also present, showing his ugly and tormented face in the form of fear or of some other giant, God's children turn back; they turn and they run away from the promised land, the land where God would give them rest, the land where they would know a new love, peace, and joy, like they have never known in their lives. This is the land where they will become a new creation, if only they cross, if only they stand up and face that which keeps them from the other side, if only they allow Jesus to set them free.

Yes, thousands upon thousands will stand on the other side, and their eyes will see the King in His beauty, and they will see the land that is very far off, just like the prophet Isaiah had written.

Yes, they will stare, and they will take in a deep breath, and then they will turn away, to return to the wilderness, to the bondage of the desert, to the darkness and coldness of its prison, to the boundaries of its captivity, all because the devil has achieved his goal in getting them to believe his lies and allow fear to consume them.

And they will look back as they are being herded back to the terror and nightmare of the wilderness by the giants that stood before them at the Jordan, and they will begin to wonder what it would have been like if only they had taken that first step. They will be herded back like a bunch of wild animals, being led to the slaughter, to their destruction, never to know what it would have been like if only they had taken the chance. Just one step away, across the Jordan, the promised land awaited—just one step away from being set free. For that was what God had promised, and God cannot lie!

This puzzled me for so long. Just what was it that held people back from taking that one step into total freedom? Just what was it that held people back from entering into a world that would be completely different from what they had ever known before, apart from the fears, apart from the sufferings? Then I began to see. I began to see after God began to reveal the bondage in which I had been held captive, after He revealed the prison I had been in and the weapons that were being used to keep me there. It was then that I began to realize how little man really knew.

What waited for people at the Jordan was the true inner person whom they had been their entire life. It was that person who had been held bound within the inner spiritual prison that had been created by the enemy during his lifetime, that person who had been held captive by the wilderness of their life.

The giants, the walls were waiting—waiting to intimidate, waiting to annihilate, waiting to create the fear that would hold them back from attempting to cross over. That fear would hold them back from taking that first important step into the waters, which would have opened up to allow them to cross over on dry land.

I began to wonder what this Jordan was that people had to cross; what was this promised land, for I really did not know. I really had no idea at the time, for I had come face to face with the enemy who had been attempting to destroy me that first day of

July, 1992, when Jesus came to set me free. I was in the very midst of the agony and torment that had me bound in the deepest part of the dungeon within my innermost being. I was still in Egypt.

Jesus had carried me through the waters of the Jordan, and when I had regained my thoughts, I was already on the other side. So I really knew absolutely nothing about crossing over, about the promised land, at least at the time. Wondrous miracles were in store for me. I would become well acquainted with the importance of crossing over the Jordan into the promised land.

At first, I knew nothing else. My life had been torment. I had thought that this was how life was supposed to be. As far as I could see, my life was normal. Everything that I did I saw as normal. I could not see anything that I was doing wrong, until...! Until that glorious day in July that the enemy was making his full attack to destroy me completely, and I cried out to a God that I had never even believed existed. Because I was hurting so much inside, because I was in so much agony and so much torment, and because God already had this planned for me, I cried out.

I thank my God so very much today that He was for real, and that He did have a plan for my life that did not include my being destroyed by Satan. I am so thankful that He heard me cry out. Because of this miracle, I had been able to see the face of the devil in my life. I had been able to see the prison in which I was bound. I had been able to see the walls that were holding me within my inner prisons. I had been able to feel the darkness and the cold that surrounded me. I had been able to feel and see the giants that were standing guard over me, but more important, I had been able to immediately feel the other side, the peace, the joy, the love.

Therefore, I had no idea whatsoever what it meant to cross over the Jordan, or of going into the promised land. What land? What Jordan? For the longest time, I had no idea, but as God began to teach me more and more through His Word, I began to understand that there truly were thousands of people who did not know, just like I did not know. It is because of these things happening to me, that God is now using me to expose those very deceptions that had held me captive.

As mentioned in an earlier chapter, even though the outer circumstances may be different, the weapons that are being used to keep us bound within our own inner prisons are identical. There is absolutely nothing different. Therefore, it is extremely important that Satan be exposed for what he is doing. The Jordan was that place of crossing that had been established by God so that His people could enter into an entirely different land from what they had ever known in their life, a land which He had established to lead His people to so that they might live in peace and harmony with each other, safe from evil. A land that would be flowing with milk and honey, productive and in abundance, for whatever they would ever need.

And all of this is given after having brought them out of the wilderness which He had led them to, after having set them free from a life of bondage in Egypt. It was all according to a plan that He had put into motion, a plan that would separate His people from the enemy, a plan in which the devil would eventually become exposed for who and what he truly was.

Today I see myself as one of those whom God has led out of the wilderness, but I had wondered, as probably many of you are wondering, what land, what Jordan? What was He talking about? But now I understand, for I am living in it today, and I am so excited to be sharing with you.

At first I had no idea that the confrontation that occurs at the Jordan was something that everyone had to experience. At least not until He began to show me the things that I would have to challenge in my life in order for me to have victory over them. It was then that I started to understand the importance of this very act if one was ever to know true freedom, for it dealt with my having to face up to the giants the devil had created in my life, which up until then had held me bound through fear and intimidation—and I can tell you that these were some really big giants!

Fortunately, my life had been in such shambles that I was willing to try anything. I had been broken. I had been defeated. I had been waiting for the knock-out punch that would end it all. Today I fully understand that only in this way was Jesus able to intercede. Where I had been looking at death, Jesus had other plans. Jesus had been thinking life, and my coming to work for Him.

Because of all this, I had absolutely no problem jumping right in trusting Jesus. Mainly because of how He had been able to take all my hurt away in one day, when I had been trying for years, with no success. I was in awe from the very beginning, and I knew that I was going to follow this Jesus no matter what. Anyone with that type of power and authority got my attention. The mere fact that He did this for me only added to my determination to serve Him. It certainly was not because I knew anything about Him, for I didn't even believe in Him at the time.

Today, I understand that this was all part of His plan for me, that this was going to be part of my preparation as I began to serve Him. Believe me, I am so excited to be able to share my freedom with you, for in doing so, I know that you also will be set free, and you will therefore know exactly what I am feeling. All I know is that you were not created to be in captivity. You were created to be a child of God and to be set free. Somehow, you are going to know this.

Crossing over is the fulfillment of God's plan for your life. Salvation comes from repenting and accepting the Lord Jesus Christ as your personal Lord and Savior. Crossing over is the deliverance from the old to the new. Salvation is not fulfilled until there has been a voluntary act of crossing over. To turn back merely keeps one as those who were not allowed to cross over, destined to die in the wilderness. God still loved them, fed them, and protected them, but when it was all over, the Bible tells us that they had to die in the wilderness.

The Bible tells us that there is life in the promised land; on the one side remains the old, and in the promised land begins the new. Jesus even led the way in what we had to do. For thirty years, Jesus lived as a man on the one side, and then He crossed over the Jordan to become the Son of God, after receiving the Holy Spirit, at which time He began His ministry. Having learned the way of man, He left all He had learned on the one side in order to begin as new in the promised land.

> Therefore, if anyone is in Christ, he is a new creation, old things have passed away, behold, all things have become new. (2Corinthians 5:17)

Accepting Christ as your personal Lord and Savior is the beginning, and is very, very important, but it is just as important to begin putting Him into your life. The only way this can be accomplished, because of the fact that we have not traveled this way before, is to leave the old so He can make you new. Therefore, crossing over is of vital importance if one is to know Jesus Christ in their personal life. A person must not only believe in Him, but they must know him.

When I was set free that first day of July, I started to believe in Him, but it was not until after I had started to seek Him out, to find out just who He was, that I began to have some understanding. What I knew in the beginning does not even come close to what He has revealed to me so far. This is why today I fully understand why one must cross over in order to be delivered. You are being delivered from the old hands that held you back, to the new hands that have been waiting for you.

The promised land is that place where we truly enjoy a life in Christ, where we have a new peace about who we are, about our life, where we feel a new love that we have never known, and a new joy that we have never felt.

The promised land is that place where one enters to experience God, that until then we had never known. This God loves His children, and wants them to remain with Him forever. Even though we continue to live here on earth as we know it, surrounded by the same trials and tribulations as we had before we crossed over, bondage has no power over us anymore. God in His magnificent power, somehow carries us through them. One literally has a whole different outlook. How, I do not know, but things are just different. God fulfills His Word.

The promised land, I can assure you, is where everyone wants to be, but in order to be there, you must choose to cross over. You must choose to be delivered from the old hands, which have held you back, to the new hands, which will take you into freedom. The old cannot survive in this land, therefore the old must die away.

What we used to know has got to go. You must look from the vantage point of the victory that has been promised you if you are to be successful, which is why to simply say, "I believe in Jesus" is not enough. You must know Jesus, if you are to have the victory which awaits only those who place their entire trust in Him. The only way to know Him is to cross over, to be delivered!

God's people had not made it very far into their life in the wilderness before God had made the decision that they would not be allowed to cross over into the promised land, a decision that was prompted by their continuous rebellion against Him. If only they would not have made God angry.

If only they would have recalled those things which God had said to them. If only they would have remembered the miracles that God had done for them. If only they would have remembered the battles that God had fought for them and won. If only...!

If only people would remember the times when they had been hungry and somehow there had always been food. If only people would remember those times when they did not think that they were going to make it, when out of the clear blue sky an answer had come. If only...!

But God heard His people complaining! God heard the words of His people. God heard them complaining, even after all that He had done for them, even after having taken them out of bondage (Egypt), and having led them through the wilderness, after having fed them, clothed them, protected them. He finally became angry!

And then they remembered! They remembered the words God had given to Moses, as they painfully had to accept their punishment for having been rebellious, for not having listened.

> ...surely not one of these men of this evil generation shall see that good land of which I swore to give to your fathers. (Deuteronomy 1:35)

I hear so many people say, "but God is a loving God, and He wouldn't let anything happen to any of His children." I totally agree, but the key word is "His"!

Those who are in rebellion to what He has commanded them not to do are saying to Him that they really do not believe in Him, therefore, how can you be "His"?

God is not the one who caused His people to rebel. He is not the one who told them to worship idols. He is not the one who told them not to believe in Him. He is not the one who told them to complain. He also never told them it would be okay to have one foot in the old, and one foot in the new. He never told them that it would be okay to do both good and evil.

The reason He never said any of these things to them is that He never meant for it to be that way. He never meant for us to worship other gods or idols, and so He became angry. He therefore established that those who were in rebellion against His Word would not be able to cross over into the promised land and would therefore die in the wilderness. Jesus so appropriately continued to make mention of this: "He who has ears to hear, let them hear." (Matthew 11:15)

But, God had a plan!! and, Jesus Christ was His name!!

God in His mercy has allowed us to be redeemed through the Blood of Jesus. He allows us to go to that moment of truth as we look over the Jordan and face up to those giants that stand before us, as we begin to make preparations to begin our journey across into the promised land. He allows us to cross over with the Word of God leading the way because we have not passed this way before; to sanctify ourselves as we prepare to cross, with the guidance and protection of the hand of our Lord Jesus Christ. For this, Jesus has come that He might be that bridge between God and man, between the wilderness and the promised land, between the desert and your heart—all so you might choose to cross over on dry land, as He becomes that bridge for you, if you will but choose.

The promised land, so close but yet so far, is nevertheless just a choice away, just a decision to want to stand up to fight for what has been stolen from you, to fight for what is rightfully yours, your inheritance, your treasure.

But, even those who had not been allowed to cross over were loved, fed and protected by God during their life in the wilderness. They were the ones who had chosen not to follow Him and therefore had to pay the ultimate price of not being able to cross over. They had been led in the wilderness for forty years to be humbled and tested, and they had failed the test.

> And you shall remember that the Lord your God led
> you all the way these forty years in the wilderness, to

humble you and test you, to know what was in your heart, whether you would keep His commandments or not. (Deuteronomy 8:2)

A lifetime in the world gives us an opportunity to find out who we truly are and to find our way back home, to find our way back to the God who created us, to be humbled and tested through our life in the wilderness so He might know what is truly in our hearts and whether we will keep His commandments or not.

What a great advantage He has given us,

...for God so loved the world that He gave His only Begotten Son, that whosoever believes in Him should not perish but have everlasting life. (John 3:16)

He gave us Jesus Christ! He gave us the way out. He gave us the bridge so that we might cross over on dry land, just as He did for the Israelites when He led them out of bondage from the enemy to the Red Sea. God had a plan for them. As the enemy approached preparing to devour the children of God, they were trapped between the enemy and the sea, and God gave them the way out. Afraid and not knowing what would become of their lives, they began to cry out to the Lord, and God heard their cries, even though they continued to complain.

Then they said to Moses, because there were no graves in Egypt, have you taken us away to die in the wilderness? Why have you so dealt with us, to bring us up out of Egypt? (Exodus 14:11)

Is this not the word that we told you in Egypt saying, let us alone that we may serve the Egyptians? For it would have been better for us to serve the Egyptians than that we should die in the wilderness." (Exodus 14:12)

And Moses said to the people, do not be afraid. Stand still, and see the salvation of the Lord, which He will accomplish for you today. For the Egyptians whom you see today, you shall see again no more forever. (Exodus 14:13)

The Lord will fight for you, and you shall hold your peace. And the Lord said to Moses, Why do you cry to Me? Tell the children of Israel to go forward. But lift up your rod, and stretch out your hand over the sea and divide it. And the children of Israel shall go on dry ground through the midst of the sea. (Exodus 14:14-16)

And I indeed will harden the hearts of the Egyptians, and they shall follow them. So I will gain honor over Pharaoh and over all his army, his chariots, and his horsemen. Then the Egyptians shall know that I am the Lord, when I have gained honor for Myself over Pharaoh, his chariots, and his horsemen. (Exodus 14:17-18)

God had a plan! You should be getting pretty excited about this, for just as He had a plan to set His people free from Egypt, He also has a plan for you! Amen! Believe me, what He has planned for you is no less exciting than what He did for the people of Israel, as they awaited certain annihilation. As a matter of fact, it is even more exciting, for it was for you that God created the way out.

Just as God honored the very words spoken by Moses as he cried out to the people in verses 13 and 14, He will also honor your words. It does not take away the fact, however, that we must still choose Him, and therefore, we must ultimately make that journey when we are called out of the wilderness. We must stand at the Jordan and face the giants before us, for Jesus wants to show us that He will fulfill what He promised you.

Unfortunately though, it is here where I have found that so many are being turned back, not wanting to make that decision to trust in a God that they do not really know. This is why just saying, "I believe in Jesus" is not enough. You are going to have to *know* Him. You are going to have to know that when you stand there looking across, you will be able to completely place your trust in Him to be that bridge for you. It is this that I have been called to do, to help you through the door, to help you take that first step.

I have found so many different weapons that are keeping so many people from crossing over, that I become very angry at the devil for what he is doing to God's people. I see him for the liar and deceiver that he is, and for the cold, callous destroyer that he continues to be.

One of the major weapons that I have found to be a major hurdle that many will have to overcome is what I call the "I know" response. This I can honestly say is one of the toughest of Pharaoh's chariots or horsemen to break, as it takes a solid grasp of the person's mind. It is called "intelligence," and it shall be defeated!

> Then the Egyptians (enemy) shall know that I am the Lord, when I have gained honor for Myself over Pharaoh (Satan), his chariots, and his horsemen (Satan's weapons and demons). (Exodus 14:18)

I will never grow weary of waiting for the breakthrough, for I know it is coming. It is already promised and will come to pass. Jesus is the one who is opening the door, and the one who is performing the miracles. The enemy cannot and will not win!!!

The Lord shall do for you as he did for the Israelites who were being pursued by the Egyptians and given a way out when the Lord told Moses:

> Why do you cry to Me? Tell the children of Israel to go forward. But lift your rod, and stretch out your hand over the sea and divide it. And the children of Israel shall go on dry ground through the midst of the sea. (Exodus14:15-16)

Yes, as Moses had a rod to stretch over the sea, you also have been given a rod. That rod is Jesus Christ, and He is saying to His children, "go forward." He is saying to you the same thing Moses told the people:

> Do not be afraid, stand still and see the salvation of the Lord, which He will accomplish for you today, for the Egyptians (the enemy) whom you see today, you shall see no more forever. (Exodus 14:13)

The enemy whom you see today, the giants in your life, the walls that have been constructed to hold you back, you shall see no more forever. Jesus is saying, no more shall the intensity of the darkness hold you back, nor its coldness suppress you ever again. No more shall the enemy exalt himself over you. No more shall the weapons stand before you.

My brothers and sisters, the Lord will fight for you, and you shall hold your peace. There is absolutely no doubt about it. Do not be afraid, but stand still and see the salvation of the Lord, which He shall accomplish for you today.

The promised land, I assure you, is well worth trusting in Jesus. Trust in Him to take you there; trust in Him to defeat your enemy; trust in Him to be the bridge for you to cross over on dry land.

The Jordan, the promised land—even Jesus crossed over to enter this land!

> And the Lord shall help them and deliver them. He shall deliver them from the wicked, and save them, because they trust in Him. (Psalm 37:40)

◆ Today Is Your Day! ◆

~ 10 ~

You Are Right Where You Are Supposed to Be

Now that you have reached that point where you must begin to look at yourself in a totally different manner from what you have been accustomed, it is so very crucial that you begin to understand that you are exactly where you are supposed to be.

Satan will now have to try to deceive you in an entirely different way, due to the fact that you are now aware of his tactics. You are also now more aware of the weapons he has been using to hold you captive, so he will definitely throw whatever he must, in order to get you to turn back. Satan is getting nervous. He is getting extremely nervous, for he has been exposed, and this gives him a lot less ammunition to deceive and destroy you. I am here to tell you that it is quite okay. He really needs to be getting nervous.

Now the tables are going to be turned. Now, all those whom he has tormented and has held captive for so many years in the depths of their inner prisons, in their darkness and coldness, are now going to begin chasing him. Freedom belongs to God's children, and freedom they shall have.

I hear so many people say, "But, I just don't think God could forgive me for what I have done." This is a clear lie from the devil himself, attempting to get you to turn back. Satan is going to try so many things, that you will have to really be on your toes to keep up with them, and the majority will deal with making you feel unworthy. He will be that little voice within you telling you that you are just too mean, or that God could never love you.

However, I am giving you a good piece of information to remember for the time when Satan makes such a thought go through your mind. If the thought has anything to do with God not loving you or not forgiving you, it is a lie. Satan has but one way to go, and that is to try to break any thoughts you may be thinking about turning to Jesus Christ. Do not accept any thought that may go through your mind that would be contrary to what you have already learned. God will not go against His Word. There is only one person who would benefit in telling you different, and it is certainly not God.

As you begin to face the challenges that will confront you, I want you to know that you have total victory over the enemy; over all the power of the enemy. Not just some, but over all the power of the enemy. He is defeated! It will be like driving into a heavy, intense fog where everything disappears, and you are straining your eyes just to see the outer white line along the edge of the road, and then all of a sudden it clears up, and your entire being seems to relax.

As you go into the smoke screens that Satan has been using to keep you blind, you will find that they will also disappear and you will know that you have been set free, if you will believe. You have come a very long way, my brothers and sisters, and I assure you that you are going to know a new you. There is absolutely nothing to fear. As a matter of fact, fear is one of Satan's weapons that is going to be destroyed forever, never for you to see again.

It will be the simple act of just turning around that will be the beginning of an entirely new world for you. If you will recall, in a previous chapter we dealt with the importance of taking that first step, and it was that first step that was the beginning of a world that you have never known before.

Oh, I am certain that there will be many who will say, "Oh, but Brother Ramón, I know all about that." Well I am here to say to you, that you do not know unless you have been in the pits of hell, in the deepest part of the dungeon where Satan holds the inner man captive so that the outer man will never know the truth about him until it is too late (for even the outer man will know after it is too late).

Unless you have felt the intensity of the darkness all around you and have had the walls literally crushed by the Rock, you can have no comprehension of what it is to be free—you just do not know!

If what you think you know has been taught to you by man, then I can assure you that you really do not know, for I am not referring to carnal or natural things, but I speak of spiritual things, and only Jesus can teach you that!

As with Joshua preparing to lead God's people across the Jordan, he had to tell them to sanctify themselves, for the Lord would be doing wonders among them. They needed to make themselves clean from all sin that was within, for they were entering into an entirely new world, over a path which they had never been before. He spoke to them of natural things when he told them to prepare provisions, for in three days they would begin to cross the Jordan (Joshua 1:10-11), and then spoke to them of spiritual things when he told them to sanctify themselves before they crossed, for the Lord was going to do wonders among them (Joshua 3:5).

God is telling His people to leave behind all that they know of the past, to leave behind its ways, its wickedness, its evil. The old must pass away, the old must die, for only when all the old has been left behind, can new take its place.

I am certain that there were many who wanted to say, "but brother Joshua, I know all about that"! The truth of the matter is that no matter what we do, where we go, or what we say, there is always a possibility that we do not know what to do, or where to go, or what to say.

All I know is that I was taken from the deepest part of the dungeon that was within me. I was taken from the cold, dark, and ugly prison that held me captive. I was released from the clutches of the giants who stood guard over me, making sure that I did not escape. All I know is that I was screaming inside, and nobody could hear me. I cried and I screamed, but nobody cared. The guards around me simply laughed, UNTIL... until that day when Somebody did hear me crying, did hear me screaming, did hear me pleading for help. All I know is that I saw the door open and a light began to shine into the prison cell where I was being held, and I heard Someone say, "take my hand," which I did!

I am so happy today to be serving Jesus. I am so very, very happy. If there are some who think that it is a sad thing to follow Jesus, then I have news for them, it most definitely is not. I am so very, very happy that I took His hand. There was a day when I, too, thought I knew all about it. I am so glad that I am not there anymore, for because of it I am free today. Once again, knowledge of carnal or natural things is not what this is all about; this kind of knowledge will keep you trapped. An entirely new world is opening up to you as you begin to deal with the giants who have stood before you, and as you see each and every one of them begin to fall.

Believe me, I am so extremely happy for you, and only you will know of what I am speaking about. No one else will understand. People will look at you in wonder and amazement, wondering what is it about you that is different, wondering just what has happened to you, but no one will ever know, UNTIL... until that day comes when you find yourself answering questions about what has happened to you. You will feel so good, and you will be so excited about the inner freedom you have that you also will feel that it just isn't fair for you to keep it all to yourself while your brothers and sisters are being destroyed. You will have been called to share your experience with others.

> Go home to your friends, and tell them what great things the Lord has done for you, and how He has had compassion on you. (Mark 5:19)

This was what Jesus told a man who had been demon possessed for his entire life and for whom He had compassion when He saw him; He immediately commanded the demons to leave him, and they left him. The man was so grateful that he was prepared to follow Jesus wherever He was going, no matter what people thought.

The people on the other hand were afraid because of what they were seeing, for they were looking at a man who had been a wild man who could not be restrained even with chains, but was now clothed and in his right mind. All they knew was what the natural mind was telling them, which was extremely limited, for it was limited to what their own eyes could see. The changed condition of the demon-possessed man created confusion in their minds, and they were unable to explain it.

How could a man bring about all this change, if he did not even know what it was that he needed to change? How could a man who was at the bottom of the barrel, defeated, rejected, with absolutely no strength left to continue, broken, and with no hope, rise up above that place where he had been? How could a man rise up above all those obstacles that were present before? There was absolutely no way. The man would need help. It was impossible for man, but not for his Creator.

So Jesus knew that it would be of major importance that the man return home to tell his family and friends and whomever else wanted to know exactly what the Lord had done for him. Only Jesus and the man could have told them about the intensity of the darkness, and about the walls, and the giants, and the coldness of the deepest part of the dungeon where he had been held captive for all of those years. Only Jesus and the man could have described the demonic activity that was happening behind the prison's walls, and about the guards that were there to hold him back.

No one else could have known. But Jesus knew that others would eventually have to know the truth, which could only be told by one who had been pulled out of the devil's clutches. Jesus knew that He would be exposing Satan for who he was, and that He would be doing it through man, for He knew that only in this way would His Father in heaven receive the glory.

Along came Jesus, who lifted him up, cleaned him up, and made him look presentable so people would see the man in his right mind, and just who would get the glory? Maybe people would not know immediately, but they would know deep down inside that a miracle had happened, and a miracle it most definitely would be! No one could have explained it. Only the person who experienced the change could explain or begin to describe what had occurred.

When it happens to you, not me, nor your father, nor your mother, nor your relatives, nor your friends, nor your pastor, nor your priest, nor your minister, nor your rabbi, nor anyone else will be able to explain it. Only Jesus and you will be able to describe the change that transpired within you, the change that made you a completely different person, and Jesus will have chosen you to be the one to tell your family and your friends what He has done for you. The freedom you will speak of will be to those who have known you. It will be to those who have seen the ugly, tormented side of you, and which they see no more. My brothers and sisters, Jesus promised you that!

I am very much aware of the demonic activity that has kept you imprisoned, for the weapons are all the same, but for me to share my knowledge of the weapons used in your life with those who do not know you will be to no avail, for they will not have known you before Jesus set you free. Jesus will be using your life, your freedom, your climb to the top, your testimony, to bring glory to His name.

Believe me, Jesus is really good! He most definitely has all of this put together very well. There is absolutely no way that I can take credit for any of the change that He brought to pass in my life. I had tried to change my life, but it never worked. Why? Because I could see only as far as my human eye would permit. My vision had been limited, therefore, my intelligence was also limited. When I thought I had it together, another weapon was thrown at me to confuse me even further. When I thought I was winning, I was really losing. My thoughts could only go so far.

Jesus, on the other hand, was watching the whole plan unfold. He had seen the weapons being formed way ahead of time and was waiting for His plan to go into action. I could have had no way of knowing that, but I am happy that I did not, for my outer being would have gotten in the way. It would have become a hindrance, for I would have thought, like always, that I knew all about it, and I would have continued losing. I just love Jesus so much. I am so grateful that He gave me the opportunity to get myself out of the way. I am so grateful that He gave me the opportunity to see Satan in action so I could just allow Jesus to pin me.

My brothers and sisters, you are just where you are supposed to be. You are exactly where God has planned for you to be, no further back or ahead, exactly where you are supposed to be. Your page has been turned to the page where God has planned from the very beginning for you to be today. It is crucial that you understand this. Once you know this and fully understand it, then Satan can no longer control you. All of his works will have been defeated, destroyed, annihilated.

"But I don't feel like I'm anywhere." That's okay, for that is exactly where you are supposed to be right now.

"But I have been a believer for so long, and I don't feel like I'm growing." That's okay, for that is exactly where you are supposed to be right now.

"But I just don't understand how Jesus could ever love me, or forgive me for what I have done in my life." That's okay, for that is exactly where you are supposed to be right now.

Whatever your perception may be, it is exactly where you are supposed to be right now, no matter what. If you are a good person, then Jesus really loves you. If you are a sinner, then Jesus really, really loves you. If you are a person who says, "but I believe in God, and I am better than that person who doesn't go to church, or doesn't tithe, or doesn't live a good life, or doesn't believe in God, or gossips, or lies, or is hateful, or is bitter, or is envious, or is a thief, or is a murderer," then I say that Jesus really wants to love you, so allow Him to break down those walls within you which are holding you back from truly knowing Him.

It will be these lies that Satan will attempt to use against you as you stand at your own Jordan looking out towards the promised land, the land flowing with milk and honey, the land which Jesus is leading the way for you to follow. The enemy will begin to tell you, "but look at all of those things that you will have to deal with, if you were to follow Jesus. People will laugh at you. People will talk about you behind your back. People will leave you."

I am here to tell you, that even if you choose not to follow Jesus right now, and if you decide not to face up to your present challenges, or to cross over, or to be delivered from the old way of life, people are still going to laugh at you and talk behind your back and leave you.

Satan tries so hard to confuse the issue. He really sees you as being stupid and not capable of seeing through his childish game. He figures that if he gets you thinking about how people are going to laugh at you, and how they are going to talk about you and how they will leave you if you decide to follow Jesus, then you will not be capable of understanding that these things are going to happen even if you do not follow Jesus.

Seriously, the worse one becomes and the deeper they are taken into their inner prison, the more isolated they will be; the more isolated they become, the less sociable they become; the less sociable they become, the more people who knew them will begin to talk about their outer problems, and the more people will begin to gossip about them. Then, the more people talk about them, the more they will laugh at them, and the more people laugh at them, the less they will want anything to do with them, for people will not want others to think they are like them. So guess what: No matter what you do, people are going to laugh at you, talk about you, and not want to be around you. The merry-go-round will continue. You will keep going further and further into your shell, your prison, your dungeon, and guess who caused all of this to happen? It certainly was not you.

Satan just does not care. He continues to use his weapons, his guards, his demonic spirits, his prisons, just to break you and destroy you. He is out to steal, and to kill, and to destroy. Are you beginning to see just how little he really does care for you? He never has! Do not allow him to deceive you anymore; see him for what and who he is. The Bible tells us that he is a liar, and you can believe that. He knows that you are on to him, so he will attempt to be even more cunning. He must, for his time is running out. He has to get you to turn back, and what better way than to get you to believe that God does not love you—lies, all lies!!

He has been doing this for so very long. Everywhere that I go, I see how he has God's children defeated. I see how he has them attacking each other, both physically and verbally. I see how he has them hating each other. I see how he has them divided against one another, and I see how he has them gossiping about each other.

Most people may think that I am referring to people in whose lives sin is obvious, and I do see many of those who are openly involved in sin, but I also see so much of this going on in the church. Not any specific church, but in the church. The church being the Body of Christ, as we are all members of His body. I hear so many things, see so many things, and the things that I hear and the things that I see are things I used to do. I was no better, but I thank my Jesus that He has set me free. Jesus has allowed me to understand something very important.

People are acting the only way that they know how. They do not know any different. I used to act like a sinner, because that was the only way that I knew how to act. It would not have mattered if I had been a member of a church, or a denomination, or a religion. I would have been acting the only way that I knew how. With this understanding, today I am able to look past the sin and look directly into the person who is on the inside. It just does not matter if they go to church or do not go to church, I still look at the person inside, for the outside will tell me an entirely different story than what is happening inside.

I am so thankful that Jesus has shown me as much as He has so far, for I have seen so many miracles happen right before my eyes, as more and more of His children are being found. As more and more of His children are being delivered. There is such a joy watching a person grow when you know that you have been used by Jesus to help bring that to pass. No one can imagine the excitement that goes through me every time I see one of those whom Jesus has allowed me to teach, advise, and counsel in His word begin to branch out and share the gospel with others, on their own.

Today, I can understand how the Apostle Paul must have felt every time one of those whom he had taught about Jesus Christ ventured out on his own to begin sharing the Good News of the Gospel. It is so very exciting. I just love it!

But, there is so much work that needs to be done. So many of God's children are being wiped out by the enemy. The deceptions are becoming even greater. The lies are being accepted with greater ease. There is no safe place, not even in the churches. I see so much hurt on the faces of my brothers and sisters who are already seeking the Lord. Wherever I go to preach, I see more and more deception; in the churches, in the streets, in the schools.

I have a friend who continuously told me about how long she had been saved. At the time, which was a little over two years ago, she used to tell me how she had been saved for eighteen years. Day after day, I heard how Jesus had come into her life, which was just great, but I also saw her break down when someone picked on her, or when one of her family members said something against her, or something devastating brought her down. Day after day, I heard about the salvation and about the good things she had heard at church, but it would never fail—something would happen to her that would bring her down. I knew even then the works of the devil, and I could see how he was holding this child in bondage without her knowing. I tried to quote scriptures that would encourage her and at the same time possibly cause her to see who she was in Christ.

Day after day, for almost one solid year (for she worked at the same place where I did), I saw her being pulled down, and day after day, I prayed to Jesus that He would cause the veil to be lifted from her eyes so she might begin to see. She was the type of person who always responded with, "I know." No matter what I shared with her about the Bible, "*she knew*"! And every night, before leaving work, I asked Jesus to please open her eyes to the truth. After a little over a year, we were at work, and the words, "I know" came up again, but this time I heard Jesus say clearly that now is the time. Almost immediately, without even thinking about it, the words shot forth from my lips, "*No, you don't know*," and I began to share the things which Jesus had shown me about deliverance.

Today, this child is serving Jesus in a mighty and powerful way. Jesus is using her to reach others she never dreamed she would be reaching. The crying has stopped, the fears have gone, and the boldness has grown. She immediately understood what I had shared with her about God's people in the wilderness and how they had to die there because they had chosen not to follow

God. She immediately understood what I meant about crossing over to the promised land, for I had shared how God's people wanted to hold onto the old, but yet they wanted to have a hand in the new.

She immediately understood that for eighteen years, she had been saying she was saved, but now she understood that she was no different from God's people who had lived in the wilderness, who had also thought they were saved because they were His people, but who ended up dying in the wilderness without crossing over to the promised land because of their rebellion. As time went on, she understood that God had a plan for her and that she was exactly where she was supposed to be. She understood that from the beginning of time, God had had a plan for her. She was exactly where she was supposed to be that day when Jesus caused her to see that she really did not know. Jesus had already moved in and needed for only the words to be said. He had already touched her, and it is the same for you.

You are exactly where you are supposed to be right now. These words are being said exactly when they are supposed to be said in your life. Neither you nor I have any choice in the matter. The pages have been turned, and you are exactly where you are supposed to be. Today, as you have read this part of this book, you have received the exact information which Jesus had planned for you. You know the works of the devil, and how he has kept you imprisoned, without your knowledge.

Pride, ego, hatred, anger, envy, bitterness, fear, intimidation, humiliation, shame, remorse, grief, mourning, anxieties, apprehensions, jealousies, selfish ambitions, all are weapons used by Satan. Every time anyone uses any of these or others, Satan is dragging that person down further into his dungeon. Over time, the person will be wiped out.

Yes, you are exactly where you are supposed to be today. You are receiving the exact words which you are supposed to receive today.

As you look at the real you, the inner you, know that Jesus has you doing exactly what you are supposed to be doing, challenging and defeating the enemy in your life. It is time to be set free. It is time to prepare yourself to cross over. It is time to remove the old, and to replace it with the new.

> Stand fast therefore, in the liberty by which Christ has made us free, and do not be entangled again with a yoke of bondage. (Galatians 5:1)

◆ Today Is Your Day! ◆

~ 11 ~

IT REALLY DOES MATTER

Deciding what direction one takes can only come through spiritual guidance from God Himself, as He begins to speak to you through your heart. Advancing spiritually requires faith, which is something one must have if they are to even think about crossing over—once one reaches the point of seriously looking at their life, wanting to move ahead because of what they are feeling inside; once one begins to seriously question the reasons why things are the way they are. Somehow, they know inside that their life is not what they had envisioned it to be, and that they are beginning to see just how they have been deceived into believing that it had been. They can now begin to see the weapons that have been used to keep them imprisoned within themselves and are wanting to have them removed from their life.

Somehow they know inside that they have been trapped by their angers, hatred, bitterness, envy, jealousies, and by many other weapons, which they never truly saw as weapons to keep them imprisoned. They never truly saw them because of the lies Satan had told them without their knowledge.

That, my brothers and sisters, is God Himself speaking to your heart. He is causing a stirring in your heart, which He is hoping will cause you to turn to Him. Which He is hoping will be the conviction which will cause you to make the most important decision of your life—crossing over the Jordan of your life; crossing over at that moment of truth as you begin to see the truth of just how Satan has kept you trapped; crossing over into deliverance.

But spiritual advancement requires faith. Just what is this thing called faith, and how do you acquire it? Just what is it that you have to do to have it activated in your life? Not knowing what faith was in my life, I jumped in with both feet when I started this journey. I had heard of the word, just like I am certain that most of you have, but I really had never had a reason to be concerned about what it meant.

Today, as I look back, my understanding of faith over the past years since I had received Jesus into my life has come because of something I had done without my even realizing it. I had jumped in with both feet. Because I did not know what to expect, or what to do next, I had made the decision that I could not do anything on my own, and, therefore, I was going to place all my trust in this Jesus, to whom I had cried out. He was able to do in one day what I had been trying to do for years.

When I saw this I began to understand what faith was all about, but this was more than just the faith that I had known in the past. It was a powerful faith. It was a supernatural faith. It was a faith that I had never known before. It was a faith that everyone must know, and it is this faith that I am being instructed to share with you.

Faith occurs when one ceases trying to do something by their own efforts and begins to trust someone else to do it for them. Faith is the one attitude that is exactly the opposite of trusting oneself. This is exactly what God is asking you to do: to cease trying to do things by your own efforts and to begin trusting in Him to do it for you, to take that step of faith knowing that He will carry you through the threshold of deliverance, into a land you have never known before.

This faith is the opposite of unbelief where one never sees beyond the trials and tribulations in their life. This faith completely wipes away all unbelief. Unbelief can never survive when this faith has made its presence known. Unbelief must flee. Unbelief causes one to look at the obstacles standing before them, rather than at God. Unbelief is that factor which Satan uses to keep God's people imprisoned within themselves, by causing them to continuously remain focused on the obstacles, in order to keep them from looking inside themselves and discovering the real enemy, Satan himself.

Supernatural faith looks at God! Supernatural faith is what we must have.

And, before anyone is tricked into a lie, which I can guarantee the enemy will attempt to throw at you, where one would say, "But I just can't do that. I just can't understand why I'm the way I am," I would like to say this: Please remember that a person can only act according to what they have been taught. A person can only act the only way they know how. The purpose of this book is to first expose the wrong that has been done against you, and at the same time to give you the ammunition to fight back.

Therefore, any thought that causes you to have doubt of any sort or to feel fear of any type is not from God. You are capable of having the faith that will be required for the advancement of your spirituality. You are capable of ceasing to do things by your own efforts and trusting Him to do them for you.

I am certain that most of you have heard different comments about the devil, or about Satan, many of them in a joking way. For example, I can recall many times when people have said, "The devil made me do it" in a joking way. Unfortunately though, little did anyone realize how true that statement really is. Therefore, I am saying this to you. Do not beat yourself up for not having known, for most truly have not known the truth. We could only act out of the knowledge we had, so you must not believe anything that is being said in your thoughts, that is being said against you. God is not against you. God loves you and He will guide you, but Satan would have you think otherwise.

Once you understand what is at stake here, and just how disastrous this game is that Satan is playing with your life, without your knowing, you will begin to see just how truly impossible it is for someone to continue to do things on their own, for these things are being done with limited knowledge while Satan is playing with technology that is way above our imagination, using weapons in such a way that you literally do not see them coming.

This imbalance of power, of course, makes the efforts we continuously summon to deal with the situations in our lives seem useless, because they are not geared for attacking the true enemy. However, we do not know this, which is exactly Satan's plan. By ourselves we can do nothing, but with Jesus we can do all things. Therefore, do not allow Satan's lies to keep you from beginning to trust in God. His technology far surpasses the devil's works. You definitely can do this!

Yes, it really does matter that people know exactly what is happening in their lives. It really does matter that people begin to see just how the devil has been exploiting them, by using whatever he has to, in order to keep them imprisoned and blind to the real truth about what his game really is, which, of course, is to steal and to kill and to destroy! Destruction may be very evident in your life already, as it had become in my life, or maybe it has just started to show its ugliness in your life, or maybe it hasn't shown itself at all—yet!

I can assure you, whether you have experienced the effects or not, the end result of Satan's game is destruction. The end result of the devil's plans is to destroy you, no matter what. It is time to begin doing the unpopular thing, to begin doing what is contrary to what the world thinks is cool, to begin having faith, to begin trusting God, and to stop trusting in ourselves. What we are being called to do by God, is exactly what we need in our lives, for His treasures include love, peace, and joy. It may seem that your whole world is falling apart around you, but inside you will have peace.

Again, the devil's technology is absolutely nothing compared to God's wisdom, but you must know how to combat the weapons that Satan will throw at you, which is why you must know the devastation that will result. Once you understand what Satan does, then he can have no more power over your life. He is literally defeated, but this is something which you must come to grips with in your own life.

Every person at some time or another must determine whether they will respond to this truth or not. Every person will have their day at the Jordan, where they will have the opportunity either to cross, or to allow the enemy to turn them back, which is why it is so very important, and why it really does matter, that one knows as much as they can about just what is happening to them before they have their day at the Jordan. Then, and only then, can one truly respond to the truth, and decide to place all their trust in Jesus.

There is a reason for the spiritual blindness which has so many of God's children imprisoned. It is this blindness which must be exposed, in order to even have the chance to respond to the truth. Unless one knows what to look for, absolutely nothing will be changed. As long as Satan continues to rule in this age, he will continue to use the same weapons he has used over and over and over again to keep God's children imprisoned through deception. It is time for him to be exposed.

Jesus Cleanses A Leper

> And it happened when He was in a certain city, that behold, a man who was full of leprosy saw Jesus; and he fell on his face and implored Him, saying, "Lord, if you are willing, You can make me clean." (Luke 5:12)

> Then He put out His hand and touched him, saying, "I am willing; be cleansed." Immediately the leprosy left him. (Luke 5:13)

The apostle Luke, who had been a physician, tells us of a man who was hurting so much from a disease called leprosy that when he saw Jesus, he immediately fell on his face and begged Him to make him clean. There had been something that this leper had seen in Jesus that told him that He could heal him of his disease, which prompted him to do what he did, and say what he had said. He knew that Jesus could make him clean, but what he did not know was whether Jesus would be willing.

Here was a man who had nothing to lose, and he took advantage of the opportunity to confront Jesus to see if He would heal him.

Here was a man who was filled with leprosy and was in so much pain that he put behind all reasons as to why he should not go to Him. The leper reached down deep into his being and found the strength to go to Jesus, even in his condition.

Here was a man who had looked beyond his condition and where he was in life to approach this man called Jesus. His desire to be healed allowed him to overlook all the obstacles that stood before him, even the way he felt about himself and his knowledge of how he looked. He had been so self-conscious of his appearance and was hurting so much, that he threw himself face down so Jesus would not have to look at him. All the poor man wanted was to be healed. The disease was slowly eating away at him from the inside out, until such time as it had progressed so severely, that the disease had broken through the skin, and was beginning to eat away at his outer being. Jesus, filled with compassion toward this man, did what He needed to do, and the man was immediately healed of his condition.

When I first had read this, I began to imagine the horror of not only having this disease, but of knowing that it was slowly destroying him. Every minute of every day, with the knowledge that this disease was just eating away at his insides, until it got so bad that it broke through the skin to expose something so ugly on the outside that people with this disease were social outcasts and sent to live in a leper colony. They were separated from the rest of society so people would not have to look at them, separated so they would just die off on their own as this slow moving disease became worse.

I imagine the torment this man must have been going through, not only from the pain of his horrible disease, but from having been shut out from the rest of the world because of it. He was basically eradicated from life, from his family, from his friends, knowing that he would never be healed, knowing that they would never have anything to do with him again.

But then, Jesus happened to be in a certain city. Jesus had been so close that this leper had been able to speak to Him. As I began to understand, it became very evident that Jesus had visited the leper colony. Jesus had happened to be in a certain part of the city. Jesus had been on a mission, and this man's day had come to have Jesus cross his path. It had already been planned. It had already been written. Even before Jesus spoke, He knew what He was going to do. Jesus did what would not have even been imaginable for anyone to do. *He touched him.* Then He said to the leper "I am willing, be cleansed." Jesus had done the unpopular. Jesus had done what most would not even think of doing.

What I began to see from this particular scripture in Luke was that even now God's children are being plagued with a form of leprosy—spiritual leprosy. A spiritual leprosy which is slowly eating away the very makeup of what God's children are meant to be, slowly eating away at the connection between God and man. A spiritual leprosy is destroying God's children today. It is a condition that ultimately causes one to feel like an outcast, just like the leper in the leper colony.

Spiritual leprosy comes in many forms. A very obvious one is rejection. Those who have been rejected for whatever reason feel lonely, left out, and not wanted. These feelings, in turn, create a very low self esteem in the individual. There is usually some outside situation, which creates a severe state of rejection on the inside, that begins to eat away at the very core of the person and eventually leads to a deeper isolation into the person's inner being, without the person having any clue as to what is going on with them. The person more than likely knows that there is something wrong, for they can feel it somehow, but they just cannot put their finger on it, and, when someone is not able to explain something, they usually just shrug it off. I know, for this is exactly what I did most of the time. It was just easier to just shrug it off than to go through the trouble of trying to discover something I knew I could not explain.

Rejection was like that slowly progressing disease, which was to become an obstacle within the person and slowly begin to eat away at the very core of the inner being, creating a loss of sensation, a loss of feeling, until it finally became a full-blown inner emotion and began to control what was going on inside that person's being.

Imagine, if you will, that moment when one has been rejected, the instant total loss of sensation, loss of feeling, complete emotional numbness, a void where one did not know what they would do. Now begin to imagine this same inner loss branching out into even more stumbling blocks as situations in the person's life become even more demanding and controlling. Loneliness begins to creep its way into the picture, a feeling of being left out, a feeling of being unwanted, a feeling of being rejected, a very low self esteem. Fear begins to overtake the person, as they have no idea what to do, and then confusion comes.

Confusion is what Satan uses to bring down the house, to keep people at odds with each other, to cause their whole inner being to shut down. All of these obstacles have but one purpose—to steal, to kill, to destroy, to basically get them to go so far down into the spiritual prison within their inner being that they would have no hope of ever being found.

The disease that would be eating away at the inner being would be so destructive, that it would seem to be eating its way through the skin, making its victims ugly on the outside—so ugly that people would begin to shun them and cause them to eventually create their own personal leper colony. They isolate themselves from the world they have known and become imprisoned in the spiritual prison that has been awaiting them.

The worse one becomes, the deeper they are taken into the dark, cold prison within their being; into the deepest part of its dungeon where no one would be able to hear them or see them—exactly the plan Satan had in mind. This condition and its destruction are so real that it is literally wiping out God's people. Just take a look around you. Just look inside yourself.

There are many, many different types of spiritual leprosy, each containing its own personal devastating purpose for the destruction of God's children. Anger, envy, pride, hatred, idolatry, sorcery, to name a few, all have the same end result—to steal, to kill, and to destroy. All these are weapons used by Satan to create the necessary illusions to keep people from discovering the real enemy, in order to keep people from knowing anything different than what he wants them to know. All of these are conditions that become part of one's life, which destroy people without their knowing. Satan does not want people to believe in God, and as long as he can keep people from believing in God, he knows that he will ultimately win. He knows that he can wait for their condition to slowly destroy them.

He gets people to begin saying that they do not have to go to church anymore, that they do not have to be a member of a church, that they can learn about God on their own. He gets people who used to do many things for the church, all of a sudden to stop doing anything as the spiritual leprosy slowly eats away at them. He gets them to become so hateful and vengeful that they become very ugly, and eventually they go off on their own into what they believe is their own little saved world.

This man whom Jesus had touched, was covered with leprosy. His leprosy was no different than many of the different types of spiritual leprosy that can be found in God's people now, eating away at them, releasing poison into the brain. Jesus wants to release His children from the leprosy that is destroying them and from the bondage that is being created by its control.

People need to get desperate enough to want to touch Jesus, desperate enough to drag themselves to Him; they need to become like the leper who threw himself down face first and humbly pleaded for Jesus to heal him. This man knew Jesus had power, but he must have felt that God would not do anything for him, as he threw himself down. He knew that he smelled and that he looked ugly, but he felt so bad that it just did not matter. He wanted to be healed. He was tired of feeling defeated. He was tired of being kept locked up. He was tired of living in isolation. Spiritual leprosy makes people believe that Jesus will not help them. It makes people lose their confidence in God. It becomes a back-and-forth faith. He will, He won't, He will, He won't.

There are many times I can recall when I had fallen prey to this deception, to this leprosy, when I had literally lost all confidence I may have had in God years and years ago. The hatred I had inside had eaten away any belief I may have had when I was growing up and eventually led me to become the ugly and mean person I had become, even on the outside. It led me to become the person who was destined to die as an alcoholic and a drug addict. That was what I had been led to believe.

God could never forgive me for what I had done. Maybe God just did not want to hear me anymore. These thoughts were all lies, all deceptions, all part of Satan's plans to bring me down and to cause me to rebel against God, but Jesus reached out His hand without reservation. He did not care what the leper looked like on the outside. Jesus touched him. He reached out and touched him. He touched him with the touch of confidence. Jesus touched before He spoke. He touched with the touch of assurance. There had been love in His touch. There had been confidence in His touch. There had been action in His touch, and He was willing.

> WILLING. Inclined or favorably disposed in mind: ready. Prompt to act or respond. Done, borne or accepted voluntarily or without reluctance. Of or relating to the will: volitional. (Merriam-Webster Dictionary)

Jesus did not desire for this leper to suffer and perish and, likewise, *He does not desire for any of His children to suffer!* But, He will not force anyone to want to be healed. He will not force anyone to choose Him. He will not force anyone to choose life. He does not desire death for any of His children, but His children must turn to Him of their own accord.

Jesus is putting radiance in His people. He is looking for a people to be holy, spotless, and clean. He is looking for a people who are willing to cross over from the old to the new, to cross over the Jordan of their life, and allow Him to cleanse them—and when Jesus cleanses someone, they remain cleansed.

Spiritual leprosy is like a cancer that eats away at the very core of the person's being, and it must be exposed if there is to be any hope of being healed. It doesn't make any difference how you're dressed, whether you are the best-dressed person in the world, or the worst-dressed person in the world. The inside is what counts. A person must clean the inside before the outside. Spiritual leprosy eats from the inside out. It is this leprosy that continues to destroy God's people. When the dirt is on the inside, it is no good. It is the inside that God is concerned about.

What good does it do to be dressed so sharp but be dirty underneath? Eventually, the person will begin to smell, and no matter how sharp they are dressed, no one is going to want to be around them. People need to clean up. The same concept applies with spiritual leprosy. What good does it do to allow the outside to say something different from what is happening on the inside? Eventually, the inside will make its way to the surface, and the truth will then be known.

It really does matter that you know and understand exactly what the enemy has in store for God's children. The weapons are all the same, and it is very important that you know, for it is only in this way that you can be healed. It is only in this way that you will call on Jesus to heal you. It is only is this way that Jesus can touch you. You must realize that Satan is a defeated foe and that Jesus' victory has been extended to you and me, which is why you must cease trying to do things by your own efforts and begin to trust someone else to do it for you, to begin to trust that Jesus can and will carry you across the threshold, as you cross over into the new you, into the promised land.

You must know who your real enemy is. You must know that Satan is the real enemy, and that you are on his hit list. Now it is time to turn the tables: it is time to put him on your hit list. It is time to do the unpopular thing. Time to do what the world would say is not the cool thing to do. Time to worry about your name being in the Book of Life, and not on the social register.

It really does matter!

Allow the Word of God to lead you across the Jordan of your life, as you stand facing what look like giants before you. I can assure you that Jesus can and will destroy them right before your eyes, if you will but trust in Him to do it for you.

> And He said, what comes out of a man, that defiles a man. For from within, out of the heart of men, proceed evil thoughts, adulteries, fornications, murders, thefts, covetousness, wickedness, deceit, lewdness, an evil eye, blasphemy, pride, foolishness. All these evil things come from within and defile a man. (Mark 7:20-23)

God knew from the beginning what Satan would use as weapons to attempt to destroy the children of God. He knew that Satan would use these weapons to cause the people to make these things a part of their life, hoping to make the people rebel against God so that God would kick them out, just as he had been kicked out of heaven. However, God had a plan that Satan did not know about. He had already made the decision to send Jesus as our mediator.

The existence of God's plan is the reason it is so important that you turn to Him now. It is time to have your eyes opened, so that you might see the truth. It is time to see that those conditions that seem like giants standing before you really are not, but simply illusions to get you to remain in the wilderness.

Yes, it really does matter!

Seek the Lord while He may be found. Call upon Him while He is near. (Isaiah 55:6)

◄ Today Is Your Day! ►

~ 12 ~

DARE TO BEGIN

Success can only come when one dares to begin, when one makes the decision, that nothing will stop them from achieving what they have chosen to pursue. There are only two ways in which one can go. Either one is for God, or they are not; either one follows good, or they do not. A person cannot do both. Either one crosses over from the old, or they remain in the old; either one dares to begin, or they stay the same. No one can be on both sides. No one can serve God and man too. No one can be for Jesus and Satan at the same time. There is just no middle ground. There simply is no in-between. There must be a separation. A line must be drawn.

It is extremely important that God's people begin to see and understand that deliverance is a must if they are to truly know the fullness of Jesus Christ. They must know that Satan will do whatever he has to in order to keep them from knowing this, including telling them that what they are reading here is all a lie.

It is extremely important that God's people know that they must cross over the Jordan if they want to go into the promised land, that the old must stay behind in order to have the new come in. They simply cannot continue to do the old and be in the new.

It is extremely important that God's people know that Satan will not tell them these things. He will only tell them lies in order to keep them on the other side while he waits for their condition to worsen. Then he can hit them with an avalanche of weapons all at once while he prepares to make the kill and destroy them.

My brothers and sisters, Satan was kicked out of heaven, and he was very, very upset about that. He was extremely angry and was determined to find a way to get back at God.

> How you are fallen from heaven, O Lucifer, son of the morning! How you are cut down to the ground, you who weakened the nations! For you have said in your heart: I will ascend into heaven, I will exalt my throne above the stars of God: I will also sit on the mount of the congregation, on the farthest sides of the north; I will ascend above the heights of the clouds, I will be like the "Most High." (Isaiah 14: 12-14)

Lucifer, the name of Satan, the devil, the angel of light, was not very happy about what God had done to him, but Lucifer had already put in his heart that he would be like God, that he would be like the Most High. However, the truth of the matter is that he was NOT! He never was, nor could he ever be! He wanted to be like God, like the Most High, which of course is something which God was NOT going to put up with. He, therefore, had Lucifer kicked out of heaven.

It is because of this, that Satan is out deceiving the children of God. He wanted to get back at God by scheming to get God to kick out man. He began searching for a way to get even with God, and when he heard about Adam and Eve, he knew what he was going to do. He was going to cause man to become rebellious and disobedient to God's instructions so that God would also deprive man from having the opportunity to be with Him.

But thank God that Satan's wisdom was but foolishness to God, for despite all of Satan's planning and scheming, God was always one step ahead of him. God, who had created all things, had known exactly what Satan would do. God had been watching Satan's every move. God had known his every thought. What Satan had planned to use in bringing about the fall and destruction of man through disobedience, God had already planned to use to cause Satan to expose himself. While Satan, in the meantime, would be thinking all along that he had succeeded in gaining victory over God, God would allow Satan to think that he was being successful.

When Satan slithered his way into the Garden of Eden to deceive Adam and Eve into eating the fruit that God had instructed them not to, his whole plan had been to shed doubt on God's word, to shed enough doubt that Adam and Eve would do what they were instructed not to do. It is this very same doubt that Satan has been using to keep God's people in bondage, generation after generation, since having first brought it into play in the Garden of Eden. Needless to say, the only way that he could accomplish this was to get you to believe his lies. By getting you to believe his lies, he is able to keep you from ever knowing the truth, until it is too late. He keeps people from crossing over without their knowledge.

I can recall many times when I would say to myself that I needed to change the things I was doing. I can recall many times when I would say to myself that this is it, I am never going to do this again. I can recall many times when I would be lying on my bed and saying that I was really going to try from here on out, but every single time it was as if I had never said anything at all to myself. It was as if those moments of self evaluation had never happened. Somehow, I had looked through all those things my inside had been saying to me that I needed to do and continued with the way I had always been, as if they had never even come up.

Though at the time I did not know what had happened, and for years after I had no knowledge of what had happened, I can say today that now I know exactly what had been going on. Each and every time that God had tried to speak to me to change, to begin doing things differently, Satan would throw his fiery darts at me. Satan would bombard me with his weapons. With all the confusion that had been going on, I would always revert back to where I had been, never giving God the opportunity to help me change. I always closed the door, not knowing any better.

Each and every time, Satan was able to shed doubt about what God was really trying to do. I could not see, nor could I hear, and with each and every time that he was able to accomplish this, I was being taken further and further from ever knowing the truth. I was being herded back into the wilderness! Even against my wishes, I was being herded back. I was being returned to where I did not want to be. As I look back at those times, and as I am writing this, I somehow feel that I knew when I was being herded back, but because I had no knowledge of Satan's lies and weapons, I was not able to put my finger on it.

I remember horrendous battles I would have within myself every time I made a mistake. It was as if a war were raging within me, and every time I screamed within myself, Why d*id I have to be this way?* Today I see where I had been at war with the demons whom Satan had been using to keep me imprisoned within myself, so that I would never be able to escape. I had fought them every single time, but every single time I lost the battle. I reverted back to where I had been before the battle, and soon thereafter, I even forget about the battle. I was being herded back into the wilderness!

What had been going on was that my inner person had been trying to escape, but because I truly knew nothing about God or what He had planned for me, I was an easy mark for Satan. Every single time I would come up to the Jordan (for that was what was really happening), I would be turned back. I was herded back to where I had come from, to where my life had been before I had tried to escape. I was held back from crossing over.

I remember yearning inside for a change in my life, but it would never come to pass. I always was herded back. The lies, the deceptions, the weapons, were all successful in what they had been sent to do—to keep me from ever knowing the truth of who I am and who I was created to be; to keep me from ever knowing the truth about an all powerful and loving God, who had been waiting for me to come back home.

I had to make the choice, I had to dare to begin. I had to dare to take the step across the Jordan. I had to dare to step into the turbulent waters that were before me before I could see that the waters would become calm.

Satan had been herding me back and was waiting for my condition to worsen so he could come in to make the kill in order to end my hopes, my dreams, and my chances of ever being with God, so he could completely destroy me, and then he would have laughed. Then he would have told me the truth. Then he would have told me how he had been lying to me my whole life.

There is absolutely no way for you to know whether what I am telling you is true unless you know what the truth is. All I know is that there has been a complete transformation of my life, and I know things now that I never knew before. I know things now that were never even brought up before. Just why is that?

If there was not a truth to be known, then why do I all of a sudden know of hidden things that had been kept from me? Why do I all of a sudden know of the total darkness which I could feel all around me inside, and of the coldness which surrounded me, and of the walls which were holding me back, and of the deepest part of the dungeon where I was being held captive, way down in the core of my inner being? How do I all of a sudden know of the void that had filled my entire being as I was falling further and further down, and of the screaming which no one else heard, and of the fear which had overtaken me?

Why? Because there really is truth, but it had been hidden by lies and deceptions to keep me from ever knowing it. Satan had truly been shedding doubt on God's word. Satan had been lying to me all along, and I would never know until it was too late and he was laughing at me, finally telling me the truth of all that he had done! But I would have now been destroyed.

The very same is being done to you. The truth is being hidden from you—the very same lies, the very same deceptions, nothing is different on the inside. The outside may be different, but the inside is the same. The very same weapons are being used: all things of the flesh, the lusts of the flesh, the desires of the heart. Your inner being is destroyed ever so slowly, dragged down further and further into the depths of the inner spiritual prison to be held captive while your condition worsens, and your condition then begins to eat away at your inside, without your knowing.

This is no game. I am seeing people being destroyed all around me. The spiritual leprosy in the form of hate, anger, and bitterness is destroying people everyday, and they are unaware that it is happening. It is time to awaken the inner person. There is absolutely no one who is excluded from Satan's plan. Whether it be the one who does not know Jesus, or the one who does know Jesus, everyone is included in his game of destruction, and the deception is getting even worse.

> Now the Spirit expressly says that in latter times some will depart from the faith, giving heed to deceiving spirits and doctrines of demons, speaking lies in hypocrisy, having their own conscience seared with a hot iron, forbidding to marry, and commanding to abstain from foods which God created to be received with thanksgiving by those who believe and know the truth. (1Timothy 4:1-3)

We are being lied to and, as it is written in scripture, we are being lied to by actual demons who are workers of Satan himself, teaching doctrines that lead to bondage, teaching doctrines that are completely contrary to what God has told His people in His word.

Unfortunately, the lies tell you that there are no deceiving spirits or doctrines or demons teaching you any of these things, even though it is written in God's word. Everything is completely the opposite from what has been told us. Everything is contrary to what God has instructed us to do. God's word tells us one thing, but we are deceived into believing that it is no longer important, that it no longer stands for what it says.

There is absolutely nothing different between you and me. Every one of our individual circumstances and situations may be different, but everything else is the same. What we are made of on the inside is the same, and what is being done to keep us from finding that out is the same.

> And the Lord God formed man of the dust of the ground, and breathed into his nostrils the breath of life; and man became a living being. (Genesis 2:7)
>
> Then the dust will return to the earth as it was, and the spirit will return to God who gave it. (Ecclesiastes 12:7)

There is absolutely nothing of importance about the flesh. All flesh was formed from dust, and to dust it will return. What does matter is the spirit within us, for our spirit will return to God. It is this spirit that will stand in judgment for what we have done, and it is this spirit that Satan is concerned about. There is something that all of us must understand. Satan is only concerned about one thing, and that is to destroy us. Even though he knows that the flesh is of absolutely no importance, he knows that this is how he must get to you. Therefore, he devotes much of his time to making sure that you will pay attention to the flesh, while he keeps you in the wilderness, never to focus on the real culprit.

By now, I pray that you are understanding just how deceitful Satan is and how much time he devotes simply to keep you from finding out the truth about your spirit. The enemy knows that is what God is interested in, for as it is written in Ecclesiastes 12:7, "...and the spirit will return to God who gave it."

That, my brothers and sisters, is what Satan planned from the very beginning after he had been kicked out of heaven. That had been his plan after learning of Adam and Eve. He had schemed that if he could get you to be as rebellious and disobedient as he had been, God would kick you out, too. It is no secret that the flesh is returning back to its original form. Dust! We all know that. We all know that when someone dies and is buried that the flesh and the bones ultimately turn to dust. It's okay that we know that. Satan is just so kind in allowing us to know that. Yeah, right!

It seems to me that he didn't mind us knowing some things, but when it pertained to his being exposed, all of a sudden it became a secret. Just look at what he has done to divert our attention from learning more about our spirit, from learning more about what God had planned for us, to keep us from learning about him.

A major weapon has been prejudice. Prejudice covers many different areas, as one can use the word to describe how they feel toward people, places, and things, based on a preconceived opinion. One can even cause another to have prejudice by attempting to sway the other person's views. Looking at prejudice in the area that is most commonly known, where it is causing the most damage because of its destructive nature, we can see that Satan has been stirring a hatred that literally controls the inner person. This hatred pulls people down into an inner prison at such a tremendous pace that unless someone pulls them out of it quickly, the hatred will literally eat him alive.

We see this prejudice or preconceived opinion literally wiping out not only the person toward whom this prejudice is directed, but also the person who holds the prejudice—and they don't even see that. Once again I say, just look around you.

These are weapons which Satan has been successfully using to destroy God's people without their knowing. They have so much hatred, anger, bitterness, envy, jealousy, selfishness, and whatever else there is in these preconceived views and opinions towards someone else, that they are not able to see that it is destroying them at the same time, because they are so intent in destroying someone else, but just whose preconceived views and opinions are they really? I tell you, Satan is really slick!

In a previous chapter I spoke of how we have received every bit of our knowledge through the views and opinions of others, and that those who shared their views and opinions with us as we were growing up had also received their knowledge through others as they grew up, and on, and on, and on, generation after generation, all the way back to the Garden of Eden.

In the Garden of Eden, there had been a great deception that caused Adam and Eve to be disobedient to God's instructions. Because of this act of disobedience, God punished them by sending them out of the Garden to make it on their own, but who was it really who prompted the disobedience? Was it not the snake who slithered his way into the Garden uninvited? Was it not Satan himself? Just whose prejudiced view was it that Adam and Eve had received? It was obviously not their own.

Now the serpent was more cunning than any beast of the field which the Lord God had made. And he said to the woman, "Has God indeed said, you shall not eat of every tree of the garden?" (Genesis 3:1)

And the woman said to the serpent, "We may eat the fruit of the trees of the garden; but the fruit of the tree which is in the midst of the garden, 'God has said, you shall not eat it, nor shall you touch it, lest you die,'" (Genesis 3:2-3)

Then the serpent said to the woman, you will not surely die. For God knows that in the day you eat of it your eyes will be opened, and you will be like God, knowing good and evil. (Genesis 3:4-5)

/ Take note just what the serpent was transferring to Eve's mind. "...and you will be like God...." This is exactly the same reason why he was kicked out of heaven. Why would one even think that it would be any different with them?

No, the views were not Adam's or Eve's. They were prejudiced by Satan's views and opinions, which were implanted and transferred from Satan to Eve and then to Adam. The order after Satan is of no importance. It could have just as easily been from Satan to Adam to Eve. What does matter, though, is that every one of you begin to see that the views and opinions were first instituted by Satan, and that this has carried on from generation to generation to generation.

My brothers and sisters, God knew this already, just like He knew what Satan would do afterwards. God knew that Satan would continue to slither his way into our lives uninvited to create havoc, torment, confusion, and destruction. God knew that Satan would slither his way into the sacred covenants of marriages, which God Himself had made holy. God knew that Satan would create weapons such as prejudice, hatred, anger, bitterness, and many, many more, in order to divert the attention of man from ever knowing the truth, to keep them from finding out about him. God knew that Satan would get people to believe that they could be like God.

Here Satan has people hating each other over something that is going to turn to dust eventually, yet he has people looking at the color of people's skin and hating each other for it, when it doesn't matter one bit. The flesh is turning to dust. He has every single color at war with each other, stealing from each other, killing each other, destroying each other. Sound familiar?

> The thief does not come except to steal, and to kill, and to destroy. (John 10:10)

What a coincidence—this is Satan himself! It is time to wake up. Satan has us zeroing in on each other, when he knows that the flesh means absolutely nothing. He has tricked us into focusing on our flesh, when it is the spirit that we need to be concerned about. God's word itself tells us that we will be returned to the ground.

> For dust you are and to dust you shall return. (Genesis 3:19b)

If God said it, then God meant it. God does not lie. It doesn't matter what circumstance or situation you find yourself in, Satan's whole plan has been to destroy your spirit, which is why he has his demons doing the work they do to keep you from finding this out. I just do not care, though. You are going to find this out, whether Satan wants you to find out or not. Satan has been slithering his way uninvited into the lives of the children of God, creating havoc and destruction. Prejudice is but one weapon, and it comes in many forms, but they all amount to the same thing—preconceived views and opinions. Rest assured, they are not your own. As much as we may not want to see that, it is the truth. Think about it. Look around you; maybe even look at yourself.

Divorces, broken homes, abuse, murders, shattered hopes and dreams, are all brought to pass because someone began to think something bad about someone else as they were being herded towards destruction. For example, let's look at divorces, which are always based on something bad about the other person. Who the guilty party is at any given time will depend on which one you are asking. In reality, however, the reason for the divorce has nothing to do with either one of them. It is caused by what is happening inside, without their knowledge or consent. It is caused by the weapons that are used to get us to do things we really do not want to do, even though we cannot understand why we are doing them. Because we cannot explain it, we simply go along. We act according to what we believe we are seeing, so we feel that it must be right.

Herded back into the wilderness! Once you start to think, you are getting too close, so Satan goes to work and pulls you back, deeper and deeper into your spiritual prison, which you cannot see.

There is prejudice between classes of people. There is prejudice between what the world sees as rich or poor. There is also prejudice between this religion and that religion, between this denomination and that denomination. It is as if this class of people or that class of people, or this religion or that religion, or this denomination or that denomination, or this rich man or that rich man, or this poor man or that poor man, have anything to do with bringing salvation and deliverance. Yet isn't that what everyone is fighting over? "Oh, I'm better." "No, I'm better." "No, we're the right one." "No, *we're* the right one."

My brothers and sisters, it's time to have our eyes opened. There is no one capable of doing anything. There is no "I'm better than you." There is no "we're right, and you're wrong." This is Satan's' plan. This is his scheme to cause people to become rebellious and disobedient to God's instructions. It is exactly what he did to Adam and Eve!

> The thief (Satan) does not come except to steal, and to kill, and to destroy. (John 10:10)

Satan does not care one bit for your flesh, other than to use it as an avenue to keep you imprisoned within yourself, and as quietly as this secret is kept, for he surely doesn't want you to know this, he doesn't care one bit for your spirit either. The only thing he cares about is that you get kicked out from having the opportunity to be with God, and from having your spirit return to its creator, God! The only thing that is right is what is written in God's word—that the spirit will return to God who gave it. This ought to get us to start thinking about just what is going to happen to us.

While this church is fighting that church, or this religion is fighting that religion, or this denomination is fighting that denomination, or this color is fighting that color, or this nation is fighting that nation, Satan is busting it. He is just having a grand ol' party with all his demon angels as they watch us steal from each other, kill each other, and destroy each other. I am not referring to the natural world here. I am not referring to stealing material things, but because of the weapons that are evident in our life, we are stealing the hopes and dreams of those around us. We are even stealing from our own selves. We are cheating ourselves out of the very gifts that God has ordained for us from the very beginning.

It doesn't matter what one is; everyone is included. It doesn't matter who you are. It doesn't matter whether you are a believer, or a nonbeliever. Everyone is still included in Satan's plan of destruction.

There are so many things being taught today that are completely contrary to what God has said in His word, and people are falling prey to their deceitfulness, unaware that they are being led to their slaughter, unaware they are being herded back into the wilderness. Unaware that they are being deceived into destruction.

> But there were also false prophets among the people, even as there will be false teachers among you, who will secretly bring in destructive heresies, even denying the Lord who bought them, and bring on themselves swift destruction. And many will follow their destructive ways, because of whom the way of truth will be blasphemed. By covetousness they will exploit you with deceptive words; for a long time their judgment has not been idle, and their destruction does not slumber. (2Peter 1-3)

False teachings, false doctrines—it is written that they will be taught by demons, teaching us to do things that are contrary to what God has instructed us to do. People are being used and are being deceived into believing that what they do is okay. Demons working through psychics, spiritists, mediums, witchcraft are all saying it is okay. They are all wanting to direct you into the future, yet they all have been marked as an abomination to God. These are not the only ones, but there will also be false prophets and false teachers in the church. The word of God tells us they will be among us. Satan's workers will even work through people in the church, without their knowledge, telling people that it is okay if they sin as long as they believe and trust in God. That doesn't even make any sense!

People are being told that as long as they continue to say that they are sorry, it will be okay. What a joke! People are being told that it is okay to intentionally sin, and that, my brothers and sisters, is not what God has said we can do. Nevertheless, that is what is being done. I know, for that is how I was living. I was brought up with the concept of different levels of sin. Sin is sin, no matter what! It does not matter how much it is disguised. Sin is sin!

The word of God is very clear as it is written:

> ...if we say that we have fellowship with Him, and walk in darkness we lie, and do not practice the truth.
> (1John 1:6)

If someone is saying that they are with God, yet they are walking in darkness, then God has said that there is no truth in that person. It is just impossible to walk on both sides of the street at the same time. A person cannot drive two vehicles at the same time. Sin is sin, regardless how much someone tries to sugarcoat it. It is just not okay!

People are being taken to the slaughter. People are being herded back from the truth. How can that be okay in anyone's book? Yet, people are being told it is okay.

My brothers and sisters, it is not okay. It is not okay to be involved in witchcraft, or with psychics, or with mediums, or with spiritists, or with demons, or to commit sin, or to do what we have been instructed not to do by God. I don't care what we are being told. It is not okay to say that you love God, and hate your brother or sister. It is not okay to say that you have fellowship with God, but still walk in darkness. It is not okay to say that you love God, and be involved in adultery or in vile passions of the flesh.

Satan has his workers all over, even in the church. Gossiping is not of God. Anger is not from God. Hatred is not from God. Nevertheless, are not these weapons found in the church? Satan is not going to let you know he is out to destroy you. He is not going to let you know that he has been lying to you. He is not going to let you know that he is going to use your flesh in order to destroy your spirit.

God's people are being taken down the tube. God's people are being taken to the slaughter—all because someone is saying that it is okay. Well, it is not okay. It is not okay that Satan is creating all of this havoc and confusion in your life. It is not okay that Satan is lying to you, deceiving you, and getting you to believe that he cares for you. Believe me, he is going to laugh at you as he tells you how he has been lying to you. The sad part is that he will tell you only after he has destroyed you. Then, you will know the truth.

I don't care who is saying that it is okay to do what is contrary to what God has told us not to do; it is not okay. The sad part is that in the end, everyone shall know the truth, one way or another. Either God will reveal it to you, or Satan will tell you all about it, after he has destroyed you.

I am angry—very angry. Angry at what Satan is doing. Angry as I look around and see all the havoc and confusion he has created. Angry at all the destruction he has created for God's children. But I am also sad, extremely sad, for most do not realize it. All I can pray is that you will just believe. Believe that God truly does love you. Believe that God really does want you to be with Him. Believe that God did send His only begotten Son to die on the cross that you should not perish but have everlasting life.

Dare to begin!

My brothers and sisters, I really do see the little children who are trapped within adult bodies, crying and screaming.—crying and screaming to be heard, crying and screaming to be set free from the dark, cold and ugly prisons in which they are being held captive without their consent.

Dare to begin! Dare to trust Jesus to carry you across the threshold, and to carry you over the turbulent and choppy waters of your own Jordan, for only He can calm the waters, and only He can set you free.

> In Him, we have redemption through His blood, the forgiveness of sins, according to the riches of His grace.
> (Ephesians 1:7)

❧ Today Is Your Day! ❧

~ 13 ~

PAID FOR BY THE BLOOD

But now in Christ Jesus, you who once were far off have been brought near by the blood of Christ. (Ephesians 2:13)

For you were bought at a price; therefore glorify God in your body and in your spirit, which are God's. (1Corinthians 6:20)

My dear brothers and sisters, what a journey you have traveled! I know, for I also traveled the same road. I know that it has not been an easy path for you to follow, but it is one that must be traveled.

Right now, I can feel the pain that many of you are feeling from having come to grips with the fact that your life has not been what you thought it was, realizing now for the first time that you have been deceived. At first, I was also overwhelmed with all the changes that were confronting me, but I can assure you that God does not give us any more than we can handle at any one time. From this day forth, there will be a freedom which you never would have dreamed possible, simply because you have chosen to confront the obstacles that have been standing in your way for so many years.

If, in fact, you are feeling the hurt and pain that must come forth when a person begins to look deep into their innermost being, I can assure you that there is a miracle right around the corner. Any time that Satan even thinks that someone is about to break out of the inner prison he worked so hard to get them in, he wastes no time in putting his soldiers to work by sending more powerful weapons which will cause them to turn back. Believe me, God will see you through all of this. God only does things that will benefit you. God only does things because He loves you. Remember that

> He who is in you is greater than the he who is in the world. (1John 4:4)

This is the reason why He sent His only Son to die on the cross for you, to give His blood once and for all, so that you could have eternal life and be with Him. Right now, you may not be aware of the treasures that await you as you step forward into a life with Jesus, but I can assure you that your journey is going to be well worth the effort you have put forth. I know that even right now, because of what you have learned so far, many new doors are already being opened. You may or may not be aware of these doors, but you will be.

There is going to be a joy you have never known—not just the joy to which most of you are accustomed, but a joy that starts at the depths of your inner being, and that causes you to shine. Before there can be this joy, however, there has to be peace. The joy of which I speak is not possible without peace, inner peace, and before you can have this inner peace, there has to be righteousness. You have to be right before God!

It is so important that God's people stop doing what they did when God took them out of bondage and led them to the land He had promised Abraham, Isaac, and Jacob. He would give the land not only to them, but to all their descendants thereafter who would believe in Him and obey His statutes and commandments. The promised land was for all the descendants thereafter who would believe in Him and obey His statutes and commandments, and this includes you and me!

Unfortunately though, the very same thing the people of Israel did back then, as they were being taken through the wilderness toward the promised land, is being done today. Even after God had led them out of Egypt and had displayed His power against the enemy, the people continued to complain. God had taken care of them, protected them, and had even performed awesome miracles to show His people that He was with them, but they nevertheless continued to complain.

That was not much different from the way it is today! Nothing has really changed. People are still complaining while Jesus has been taking care of us without our knowing. He has been protecting us and is still most definitely performing miracles in the lives of His children to show them that He is with them in hopes that they will turn to Him. Nevertheless, we still complain. Nothing has changed.

The promise that God made to Abraham, Isaac, and Jacob is still in effect today for us, as it was for the people of Israel. The same promised land the Israelites had to look forward to is still available to us. The same words spoken, the same protection, the same love, is still available for us today, and it has been throughout time. However, just as all of the above are still available, so also is the price one will pay for rebellion and disobedience.

> Now it shall come to pass, if you diligently obey the voice of the Lord your God, to observe carefully all His commandments which I command you today, that the Lord your God will set you high above all nations of the earth. And all these blessings shall come upon you and overtake you, because you obey the voice of the Lord your God. (Deuteronomy 28:1-2)

> But it shall come to pass, if you do not obey the voice of the Lord your God, to observe carefully all His

commandments and His statues which I command you today, that all these curses will come upon you and overtake you. (Deuteronomy 28:15)

This message is very simple, very plain, very concise, and very true, and just as God fulfilled His word to the Israelites, whom He had brought out of bondage, by not allowing them to cross over into the land which He had promised them, so does He still fulfill His word today. If we rebel, then we will pay, but if we obey, then we are blessed.

All I ever ask people to do is look around them, to think about their own life. When they are doing something wrong, things go wrong, but when they are attempting to do good, things seem to go well. God is still fulfilling His word today! There is no question about that!!

We shall either be with Him, or we shall not. What a great and awesome God we have, who allows us to choose. What a great and awesome God we have, who gave us an even greater opportunity to be with Him, which the Israelites did not have.

The Blood of Jesus!

The Blood of Jesus was what Calvary was about. The Blood was what the cross was all about. The Blood was what victory was all about. Yet, Satan has deceived people so much that most have no idea whatsoever what the Blood of Jesus really represents. These are merely words to the one who is lost. These are merely words even to the church, to those who say they have fellowship with Him, but yet do not really have any clue as to its meaning, other than what they have heard. How do I know? Because I was one of those who had been lost. I was also one of those who was in the church at one time, but I had absolutely no idea what they were saying when they spoke of the blood. As a matter of fact, very rarely can I recall that the word *blood* was even mentioned, except when it was read for communion purposes, but there was never any understanding of its meaning.

And I know that many would say that I was not listening, but I was listening. How else would I know when the word was used. I just did not have any understanding of what it meant, and because of that, I became an easy mark for Satan to pull me away from the church many years ago. I did not know about what Jesus had done for me. I did not know what His purpose was for me. I did not know exactly why He died for me. Sure, I had heard all about these things. I had heard about Jesus. I had heard about the cross. I had heard about the blood. I had heard about heaven. I had heard about God. I had heard about angels. I had heard about good and evil.

I had also heard about sin. I had heard about mortal sin. I had heard about venial sins. I had heard about hell. I had heard of a purgatory. I had heard about the fire. I had heard about the devil. I had heard about a God who wanted to punish me.

None of it made any sense to me. All I knew was that I really did not care to know this God who wanted to hurt me. Maybe I will be the only one to admit this, even though I do not believe that I am the only one who has ever felt this way. I really and truly did not know. I really could not understand any of this.

Many will say that they knew what all of this was about, but I would have to ask, did you really? For if they really knew, then why is there so much strife and conflict in peoples lives? Truly understanding what Jesus did would eliminate any feeling or emotion from within that is not of Him. The trials would all still be there, but they could not bend Jesus within them.

I am so thankful to Jesus for having cleared this up for me, for today I do know what I have because of the Blood of Jesus, and He has made it very clear to me that everyone needs to know exactly what His Blood represents. For it is this Blood that guarantees us the victory over the enemy, the only enemy we have, Satan. Without it, there is no victory, there is no freedom, there is no light. But thanks to the all-powerful, mighty, and awesome Father of our Lord Jesus Christ, we do not have to concern ourselves with any of that, for there is already victory. There is already freedom. There is already light—all because of the Blood of Jesus!! All we have to do is accept it. It is this which I will now share with you.

The Blood of Jesus!

This is most definitely my favorite subject today. I have my freedom because of it. I have a new-found peace because of it. I have a new-found love because of it. I have a new-found joy because of it. I have my family because of it.

You must understand that I had been on the verge of losing what was the most important to me at the time—my family. Everything else meant absolutely nothing, and I have no doubt whatsoever that without Jesus I would not have them today. What I have learned over the past four years is that Satan cannot stand to even hear about the Blood of Jesus. Needless to say, he cannot stand knowing that the Blood of Jesus continues to defeat him. There is absolutely nothing that Satan can do to even attempt to bring someone down who is covered by the Blood. This is why it is so important that everyone know exactly what it represents, and how powerful it is in their life, and this I can assure you is something that Satan does not want you to know, but the good news is that there is nothing he can do about it.

Paid for by the Blood, just what does that mean?

Of all the things I have been given the opportunity to understand by Jesus, I would have to say that the most precious and most valuable has been about His Blood. The most important subject that Jesus is prompting me to share is about His Blood. He knows that His Blood is the tie between God and man, that His Blood is what binds the covenant that is being made with you. This is God's way of saying to you that He will honor His commitment to you if you will but fulfill your end, if you will do what you say you will do.

I want to say that I had absolutely no comprehension of what Jesus did for us at Calvary, but it was there that the victory took place. I believe that most people do not really know what happened at the cross, even though they say that they do. I say this because I hear people say so many times, "I just can't understand why so-and-so keeps doing the things he (she) does, knowing what Jesus did for them." I truly believe that people do not know what Jesus did for them, for if they really knew, there would be a change in who they are.

A person is only capable of acting according to what they know, which is why they can continue to do things which are frustrating to someone else who thinks that they should be acting differently. The truth of the matter is that the person is acting out exactly the way they are supposed to be, based on what they know. In their eyes, they are doing the right things. Believe me, I know this because I thought I had been doing things right. Therefore, if someone is to begin experiencing a change in their life, there must ultimately be a change in their thoughts.

Most people have heard of how Jesus had been turned over to the Romans to be crucified, and of how Pilate had wanted to wash his hands of the whole affair, but because of the persistence of the Jews, he released a notorious prisoner called Barabbas and sentenced Jesus to be crucified, just to make them happy.

Most people have heard of how Jesus had a crown of thorns placed on His head, in order to humiliate Him and of how Jesus was forced to carry His cross through the streets on His way to a place called Golgotha—Place of a Skull—where He was to be nailed to the cross to die.

Most people have heard of how Jesus said as they placed Him between two robbers, one on the left and one on the right,

> Father, forgive them, for they do not know what they do. (Luke 23:34)

Most people have heard of how the Roman soldiers cast lots for His robe, and of how they mocked Him, and of how they eventually put a spear in His side.

Yes, most people know all of these things, because they have either heard them from someone else or were taught them in a religion class or heard them on television on one of the many programs that have been made about Jesus being crucified. But, that is as far as it goes. I believe that just because someone has knowledge of something does not mean that they have an understanding of it. It is not that they cannot understand what Jesus did, but they have never had anything explained to them for them to understand. There is a difference.

For example, I am writing this book on a computer. Prior to my beginning to use the computer, I had been writing this book by hand, and then I had planned to use a typewriter, but my son talked me into purchasing a computer. I had heard about computers through hearing others talk and from what little I had seen on television, and I can say I had very little knowledge of them. I did have a little kowledge because of what I had heard, but it did not mean that I understood what was being said! I was not fully acquainted with the operating functions of a computer, and by no means could I have considered myself to be an expert in its use.

Computers were foreign to me, but because of the patience which my family has shown to teach me what they know, I now have a basic understanding of how computers work, which allows me to use the computer whenever I choose, and I can type these words onto a disk. What I have is not full knowledge, but it is enough to allow me to begin so I might learn more. It is no different with Jesus, with the Cross, or with the Blood.

If someone had taken me and sat me down, and began to slowly explain to me word for word what Jesus had done for me with the same love and patience my family extended in showing me how to operate the computer, I am certain that I would have had a greater understanding of Jesus. But, it is never this way.

People are concerned about this, or about that. People are in a hurry to do this or to do that. They say, "Besides, I have a job to do, and I have to go to it in order to pay my bills and feed my family. Therefore, I really do not have the time to slow down and hear what you have to say to me. Besides, maybe I'll get the chance to go to church on Sunday, and it will all be explained to me during the hour that I am there."

Sound familiar? I was there. This was what life had taught me. It was not like what people were saying to me. "Where were you when they talked about Jesus? You just weren't listening, were you?" I'm not attempting to defend myself, for it really does not matter now, but I really was listening. I really was there. It just did not make any sense to me. I really believe that if I were to go around asking people today, "Would you please explain to me exactly what Jesus did for me and just what does the Blood mean?" I am positive that the majority would not be able to answer me. Why? Because no one can talk about something that they do not know anything about. It really is true. Of course, someone can pretend that they are saying a lot, but if they really do not know what they are talking about, it will show. Others will pick up on it.

I am not saying any of this to belittle anyone, for if there is one who truly does not know anything, it is I, but, it is important that you begin to see just how deceiving Satan really is. It is important to know that the majority of those who were doing the teaching really did not know themselves, so how could you really know? There are pastors, ministers, priests, and other religious people who have been entrusted to shepherd God's children today who really do not understand themselves. How do I know, because I have asked some of them. They can tell you about what Jesus did, and about the word of God, which they have read, but it escapes them how to explain exactly what it really means.

I am not saying that I know everything, for I know absolutely nothing, but God's Holy Spirit is the one who reveals all truths, and He is allowing me to share what He has placed in my heart—what He has placed in my heart to share. Without Him I could do nothing, I would know nothing. It is only with Him that anyone will ever know anything. If you will recall what I wrote about Satan's weapons that are used to keep us from knowing the truth, this should explain why the truth is not always known, even by those whom we would think should know.

For you see, Satan does not care who one is, or what title one has; he is going to deceive you, to keep you from knowing the truth. Does it stand to reason that Satan would want to attack those who are preaching the word of God to others? If Satan were able to deceive them into not knowing the entire truth, how could those who were listening to them ever know the real truth? Doesn't this make sense?

I am not saying that these pastors, ministers, priests, or other religious people are bad, but I am saying that we are all in the same boat. Satan is out to steal and to kill and to destroy, whether you have a title in front of your name or not. We are all included. It is so important to remember that everyone has views and opinions that have been passed on from the views and opinions of others. These include religious and doctrinal views that have been taught generation after generation after generation since the beginning of time.

All religions and denominations had a beginning at some point, and most came about because of differences in their views and opinions from each other, views and opinions that were passed on through teachings and doctrines that were originated by views and opinions given by man. Is it possible that Satan may have infiltrated their views and opinions along the way? It is not only possible, but he has. This question is really not hard to answer. All we need to do is to look at all the discord that exists in the church today. There is so much confusion, backbiting, hatred, anger, gossiping and fighting going on in the churches today. *None of these are of God!*

Man can be deceived. God cannot! Jesus is bringing an awakening to the church. Jesus is making it known that the church is to look to Him only. Jesus is making it known that He is the church and we are all members of His Body. It's time to wake up church, it's time to arise and shine!

This is happening every single day. Satan is stealing the word of God more and more every day, and people are getting further and further from the truth. The churches are beginning to accept more and more of what the world is doing, even though it is totally contrary to what God has said in His word. If God said it, then that is what He means. It's not, "Well, I think He meant to say this or that in His word." God is not a God of confusion, but of love and of a sound mind. He knows exactly what He said and what He meant by it. Twisting the word of God benefits only one person—Satan. It was Satan's plan all along to shed doubt on God's word, because he did not want to go down alone.

But, there are no two sides. Either you ride high with Jesus, or you allow Satan to take you down with him, which by the way has been his plan for you from the beginning, and I believe that this is all happening because there is no understanding of what Jesus really did on the cross.

I thank God that He has given us the opportunity to listen to Him. I am so thankful that He did not just wipe us out, but instead gave us a way out. I am thankful that He sent His Son to die on the cross for us, that He sent His Son to shed His blood once and for all so our sins would be forgiven, and that we could have eternal life with Him.

The question is not "does God want to accept you," but "do you want to accept Him?" He has already shown His desire for us by sending His Son to die on the cross. Now the question becomes, "Do you want to accept Him as the truth?" God is bestowing His wisdom and knowledge upon His children as He begins to expose the works of Satan, as He begins to draw His children even closer to Himself and begins to reveal the mysteries of His Word—all through the Body and Blood of Our Lord Jesus Christ. Whether Satan wants you to know it or not, you will know just how precious and valuable the Blood of Jesus really is in your life. The Blood that Jesus shed on the cross was all for you!

> But Christ came as High Priest of the good things to come, with the greater and more perfect tabernacle, not made with hands, that is, not of this creation. Not with the blood of goats and calves, but with His own blood He entered the Most Holy Place once for all having obtained eternal redemption. (Hebrews 9:11-12)

From the time when God had given Moses the ten commandments to give to the Israelites at Mount Sinai, a covenant was made between God and Moses that would allow the priests who had been chosen by God to make animal offerings. These offerings were intended to bring temporary relief to man's guilt and to demonstrate the lessons of God's justice. The covenant through Moses provided a bond in the blood of the animals. The only stipulation was that these sacrifices had to be performed each and every year. This was the way God had agreed to in the covenant that would allow man to seek His forgiveness.

However, a second covenant was deemed necessary by God.

> For if that first covenant had been faultless, then no place would have been sought for a second. (Hebrews 8:7)

> Because finding fault with them, He says: "Behold, the days are coming, says the Lord, when I will make a new covenant with the house of Israel and with the house of Judah—not according to the covenant that I made with their fathers in the day when I took them

by the hand to lead them out of the land of Egypt; because they did not continue in My covenant, and I disregarded them, says the Lord." (Hebrews 8:8-9)

For this is the covenant that I will make with the house of Israel after those days, says the Lord: I will put My laws in their mind and write them on their hearts, and I will be their God, and they shall be My people. (Hebrews 8:10)

Because the first covenant had set the standard for living under God's rule but did not provide the power to keep the laws of the covenant, God established a new personal covenant relationship with His people. This time, however, not only would His laws be implanted in the minds and hearts of each and every one of us, but He would also provide the power to allow those who believed in Him to keep them. This power was He of whom He spoke in John 14:16-17:

And I will pray the Father, and He will give you another Helper, that He may abide with you forever—the Spirit of truth, whom the world cannot receive because it neither sees Him nor knows Him; but you know Him, for He dwells with you and will be in you.

And in the very next verse Jesus said:

I will not leave you orphans; I will come to you. (John 14:18)

This power, which God after seeing that His people would need help to combat the weapons that Satan would continuously throw at them to cause them to be rebellious and disobedient, was His Holy Spirit, and the only way in which the Holy Spirit could come was by Jesus Christ leaving.

Nevertheless I tell you the truth, it is to your advantage that I go away; for if I do not go away, the Helper will not come to you; but if I depart I will send Him to you. (John 16:7)

God most definitely had a plan to do away with Satan, but the plan still would require that each and every person make a choice.

> None of them shall teach his neighbor, and none his brother, saying "Know the Lord" for all shall know Me, from the least of them to the greatest of them. For I will be merciful to their unrighteousness, and their sins and their lawless deeds I will remember no more. In that He says, "A new covenant," He has made the first obsolete. Now what is becoming obsolete and growing old is ready to vanish away. (Hebrews 8:11-13)

I pondered on these three verses for the longest time before I realized what they were saying to me. God was basically telling me that He had placed His laws and commandments within me from the day that I was born, but I needed to find them. If I did find them, He would be merciful to my unrighteousness, and to my sins, and my lawless deeds He would remember no more.

Yes, I was confused, but as I began to seek the kingdom of God, He began to make His word clear to me. He has allowed me to begin to understand. He reminded me of all the times when I wanted to do something that I knew inside was wrong, but I went ahead and did it anyway. Every single time I was warned internally that I should not do it, but I did it anyway.

It was then when I realized that God's laws and commandments had been within me from the beginning of my life, but I had had to find them. Once I found them, I began to seek for more knowledge of what I had found, and I began to realize what Jesus had done for me. The first covenant had set the standard of how I was to live, but it was the second covenant that provided the power to keep them. Once I knew who God was, He was then able to fulfill His promise to me.

> For if the blood of bulls and goats and the ashes of a heifer, sprinkling the unclean, sanctifies for the

> purifying of the flesh, how much more shall the blood of Christ who through the eternal Spirit offered Himself without spot to God, cleanse your conscience from dead works to serve the living God? (Hebrews 9:13-14)

> And for this reason He is the Mediator of the new covenant, by means of death, for the redemption of the transgressions under the first covenant, that those who are called may receive the promise of the eternal inheritance. (Hebrews 9:15)

Your receiving the promise of the eternal inheritance was of major importance to Jesus. He wanted you to receive and was willing and obedient to His Father to go all of the way to the cross. Jesus knew that He had to die in order to accomplish this! Even Satan knew that Jesus must die, which is why he tried ever so hard to get Jesus to fall during his three-year ministry, after Jesus had crossed the Jordan. But God had prepared Jesus for thirty years prior to His crossing over the Jordan, to get to this point—the Cross. Jesus was prepared to die on the cross. Jesus was prepared to deal with all the weapons Satan would throw at him.

> And Jesus increased in wisdom and stature, and in favor with God and man. (Luke 2:52)

Yes, Jesus knew that He had to die on the cross in order to ensure that you receive what His Father had promised to you.

> For where there is a testament there must also of necessity be the death of the testator. For a testament is in force after men are dead, since it has no power at all while the testator lives. (Hebrews 9:16-17)

For example, if you were making out a will (testament) to leave to your children all that you had accumulated during your life as an inheritance, what would you have to do in order to put this will into effect? It is obvious that you would have to die, for as long as you lived, the will (testament) would be of absolutely no value to those whom you had named as beneficiaries in the will. The same holds true with what Jesus had to do, for as long as He remained, His Holy Spirit could not be sent. Jesus had to die and shed his blood so that you might receive all that was left as an inheritance to you, and because the covenant was instituted by God, it was required that blood be shed, for this was His word.

> Therefore not even the first covenant was dedicated without blood. For when Moses had spoke every precept to all the people according to the law, he took the blood of calves and goats, with water, scarlet, wool, and hyssop, and sprinkled both the book itself and all the people, saying this is the blood of the covenant which God has commanded you. (Hebrews 9:18-20)
>
> Then likewise he sprinkled with blood both the tabernacle and all the vessels of the ministry. And according to the law almost all things are purified with blood, and without shedding of blood, there is no remission. (Hebrews 9:21-22)

Remission is to send away. The word signifies a release from bondage or imprisonment, dismissal, sending away, and forgiveness, with the added quality of canceling out all judgment, punishment, obligation, or debt.

Bingo!

Paid for by the Blood! Jesus was the mediator to make certain that you received all that was promised to you by His Father. The blood was the ultimate price one could pay to bind the covenant which God had made. The death of Christ was a necessity. Apart from the shedding of the blood of Jesus Christ, there is no remission, no forgiveness. The shedding of the blood has released you from the inner spiritual prison in which Satan has been holding you captive, from all bondages, from all imprisonment. All the debt owed has been canceled. The blood of Jesus has made you debt free.

Then He adds, "their sins and their lawless deeds I will remember no more". Now where there is remission of these, there is no longer an offering for sin. (Hebrews 10:17-18)

You, my brothers and sisters, have been *Paid for by the Blood!*

These things I have spoken to you, that in Me you may have peace. In the world you will have tribulation; but be of good cheer, I have overcome the world. (John 16:33)

◄ Today Is Your Day! ►

~ 14 ~

STAY IN THE FATHER'S HOUSE

Looking back over my life, I see so clearly the difference between how my life used to be and how it is now. There is a dramatic change in how I handle situations today, compared to how I used to handle them. The changes that I went through, the emotions that I battled, are all so dramatically different.

Blessed be the God and Father of Our Lord Jesus Christ who has so much love to give to His children that He never gave up on me. I am so thankful and grateful for the gifts He has bestowed upon His children, for without them I know that I could have never experienced the joy that I know today, the peace that I know today, the love that I know today.

I am even more thankful and grateful for the plan that He had already written for my life, before there was even one. I am so thankful that He chose us in Him before the foundation of the world, that He predestined us and has redeemed us through His blood.

I am so thankful for all of you, for Our Father has included your lives in His master plan for me. The plan in my life came about because of the plans He had for your lives. Yes, I am indeed very thankful and grateful.

Our Father knew the obstacles that would cause us to stumble. Our Father knew who the enemy would be. Our Father knew the weapons the enemy would use against us. Our Father knew what He had decided to do.

It is no wonder why I have chosen to stay in the Father's house, in my Father's house, in your Father's house. In the house where Our Father protects us. In the house where there is never any need. In the house where we are the children. In the house where we are loved with a love we have never known before. In the house where there is joy. In the house where there is peace. In the house where evil has no power.

I have already tried living miserable, being filled with fear, hatred, anger, bitterness, torment, and destruction for way too many years! What a joy it is to be able to choose; to be able to choose between life and death; to be able to choose between doing good and doing evil. It is a whole new world. I have not left, but yet I have something totally different from what I had ever known before. The separation, the difference has all been within, but it is that change within which is now creating a change without, and I know exactly why this is so!

> Now it shall come to pass, if you diligently obey the voice of the Lord your God, to observe carefully all His commandments which I command you today, that the Lord your God will set you high above all nations of the earth. (Deuteronomy 28:1)

I have chosen to remain within the Father's house. I have chosen to diligently obey the voice of the Lord my God. I have chosen to observe carefully all His commandments. I have made the decision to walk in His ways!

Before, I had thought that I had been free. I had thought that I had been in control of my life. I had thought that it was I who made things happen or not happen. How wrong I had been!

FREE. Having liberty. Enjoying political or personal independence. Not subject or allowing slavery. Made or done voluntarily; spontaneous. Relieved from or lacking something unpleasant. Not subject to a duty, tax or charge. Not obstructed; clear. Not being used or occupied. Not fastened. Lavish. Open, frank. Given without charge. Not literal or exact. Not restricted by conventional forms. (Merriam-Webster Dictionary)

This is hardly what I had thought when I used to say I was free. *Having liberty.* Yet I was being held in bondage. I was being held imprisoned without my knowledge.

Not subject or allowing slavery. I was being controlled by the weapons which were being used in my life to keep me in bondage or in slavery.

Made or done voluntarily or spontaneous. I had been deceived into believing that I was the one who was making the decisions, when in fact they were being influenced by the situations or circumstances which were in my life. And on, and on, and on.

What an awakening one can have when one begins to seek the truth. How sad, though, that most will never seem to have a reason to want to seek it until it is too late, like it had almost been for me. Or was it that I was also being led in a different direction all along so that I would never think that I did not know the truth?

It really does not matter anymore. Today I understand what true freedom really is. I know what it is to be free, and I can assure you that it is not what I had thought it was before, which is why I chose to stay in my Father's house. I have known the love, peace, and joy that the world has to offer, and I guarantee you that it just does not compare to the love, peace, and joy that I have today in Jesus. This is for me. This can only come through a personal relationship with Christ. Only He can extend this to you. I can only share what it is that He has given me.

You can never know if what I am saying to you is the truth unless you know that there is a truth to be known, and that can only come from the Father of our Lord Jesus Christ. I would never even attempt to argue the point with anyone, for I know that what I have been shown is because the Father of our Lord Jesus Christ wanted me to know, and the same would hold true for you. Therefore, I will only share what I have been instructed to share: what the Lord Jesus Christ has done for me.

Having tried both sides already, I know which side I prefer. I am thankful that God has given me the ability to be able to make a choice, to be able to say that I choose to be free, to be able to say that I choose to live, and comprehend what I am saying. I am grateful to be able to say that I choose to stay in my Father's house, and mean it.

The change I am talking about is not just about repenting, being baptized in the name of Jesus Christ for the remission of sins, and receiving the gift of the Holy Spirit, though this is the beginning. This is extremely important, for without Jesus no one can even think about crossing over, but there is so much that must be done.

There is another side. It is also about going forth to experience the fullness of the Holy Spirit, God Himself, in your life,. This can only come about through deliverance, deliverance into the Promised Land—not just partial deliverance, where one wants to believe that they have been delivered, but full deliverance into the Promised Land.

Full deliverance is deliverance that will have come about because of the decision that was made as one stood at the Jordan of their life, their moment of truth, looking out into the choppy, turbulent waters, with its powerful and horrendous waves coming towards them looking as if they were ready to destroy them. With absolutely no comprehension as to how or why, refusing to listen to what was being said to them, even through all the fear that was beginning to consume their very being, they stepped into the waters.

This is the place where most of God's people are turned back, the place where within themselves, they believe that they have been delivered because they have made it to that point. This belief deceives them, and they are turned back, thinking that all is well, only to be continually plagued with the same bondages from which they thought they had been delivered.

There are so many of God's children who are yearning to know the fullness of God, who are yearning to be completely set free from the bondages which continue to remain in their lives years after having repented, after having received Jesus as their personal Lord and Savior. They cannot understand why.

They could not understand why they have not yet had these bondages removed from their lives, and why they continue to struggle in the very same areas from which they had believed that they had been delivered—especially since they had already done what the word of God had said, or so they believed! As time continued to pass, they began to think that God had turned His back on them!

But it wasn't that God had turned His back on them. The persistence of their bondages came from the specific weapons the enemy had put into action to use against them. These weapons were carefully chosen according to what he thought would cause them to stumble, even if it meant to get them to believe that they had been delivered. The enemy just does not care.

Remember that when you are on the verge of crossing over, at that moment of truth, the enemy will throw whatever he has to in order to get you to turn back. Once he has you turned back, he can wait for your condition to worsen before he ultimately destroys you. So, if he has to, I can assure you that he will throw the weapons which are of importance to you, like your being told that you are delivered. Satan will definitely deceive you.

God desires that we should be holy and without blame before Him, not having spot or wrinkle or any such thing. He is desiring for us to be without blemish. He has given us the way to follow, but He will not push you to take part.

Everything must be left behind. You must cross with absolutely nothing. Nothing can be held back. He will know.

Everything must be left behind. You must cross with absolutely nothing. Nothing can be held back. He will know.

This is so important for you to know that it needed to be repeated. So many times, people reach the point of crossing and think that they will be able to hang onto something and God will not know about it. It is like when Adam and Eve were hiding from God when He had called out to them. They knew that they had done wrong, and the last thing they wanted was to face God. What they did not realize, though, was that God already knew what they had done. He knew that they were trying to hide it from Him, but He waited for them. He waited for them to tell.

We try to keep just one little piece of our life, that will keep us in touch with what we understand as a human. Often we don't even know we are doing it. No one is excluded. I was just as guilty as anyone else. I had been deceived into thinking I could hide from God, just like everyone else, but no more! I do not want to ever be hidden from the presence of God again.

There is absolutely nothing in or of this world that is worth losing the opportunity of being with Him, and Satan knows that, which is why he tries so hard, and throws so many weapons at you, to keep you from ever finding that out. God will not force anyone to do something that they choose not to do. If they choose to try to hide something, He will let them, but then without their even knowing, they are opening the door for the enemy to use deliverance as a weapon, when in fact, nothing has been accomplished.

Maybe there is only one little thing that is being held back, but it may as well be thousands. It's not the one little thing that will hold you back—it is the fact that you still are attempting to maintain control, and God will not overstep your desire. He wants you to be with Him—your whole you, not just part—but He wants you to make that decision. As long as you choose to remain the pilot in your life, God will not stop you. *Everything must go!*

> Therefore we also, since we are surrounded by so great a cloud of witnesses, let us lay aside every weight, and the sin which so easily ensnares us, and let us run with endurance the race that is set before us. (Hebrews 12:1)

Let us lay aside every weight, and the sin which so easily ensnares us! The apostle Paul is warning us to get rid of every sin (weight) that holds us from approaching the throne of God, including the sin that so easily ensnares us. He is telling us that we must search and search to make sure that every sin is exposed. Paul knew that nothing could be left behind, for God would know. He therefore cautioned the Hebrew church to rid themselves of every weight. Anything that was not of God, was not worth keeping.

Thank you, Father, for the word that You have just given me.

God is saying that He has said in His word, that if anyone is in Christ, he is a new creation; old things have passed away, behold all things have become new. He is saying that if you are not willing to let all the old pass away, then you are not in Christ. For if you were in Christ, then you would be a new creation, for then the old things will have been exposed and dealt with, and therefore the door will have been opened for Him to take you across, where all things will have become new. God is saying that as long as you think that you can approach His throne without having dealt with every single weight which holds you back from being delivered, that the enemy will continue to have his way. And the reason will be because you have tied His hands from moving in your life, by your even thinking that He could be fooled.

Thank you Jesus!

Once this has been done, then Paul tells us to run with endurance the race that is set before us. If this is not done, then the weight itself will be so heavy that it will be impossible to run any race, except to be turned back. To encourage God's children to be diligent and sincere in exposing all sin, he tells us that we are surrounded with a great cloud of witnesses. It is not that these witnesses are looking down at us, but he is saying that many have gone before us and have crossed over after having laid aside every weight, so Paul is assuring us that we too can do this.

Believe me, there is no such thing as partial deliverance. Just like there is no such thing as deliverance while you are still the pilot, while you are still at the controls. If you believe that you can still have deliverance while maintaining control, then I assure you that God is not the one sending the message. God will not lie to you.

You cannot allow the enemy to trick you into believing that you can continue to do what the world is saying is okay but is contrary to God's word, and still be delivered. For without Jesus leading the way, you cannot cross over. I do not care what you are being told. *Jesus did not say that He might be the way, He said He is the way!*

I encourage you to read about the journey of God's people in the wilderness. They had been deceived into believing that they would be allowed to cross over into the promised land while continuing to be rebellious and disobedient to God's word. They never got off the train. It kept going, and going, and going, until time ran out on that train. The end result was destruction, annihilation. The journey that is found in Exodus, the journey that begins with God bringing them out of Egypt (bondage) and continues through the wilderness, was a time of testing. It was a time for God to find out where their hearts and loyalties really were.

Jesus gave us a very good example of just how much His Father loved us and of the concern He has for us. He told a parable of two sons, and of how one had chosen to go off on his own.

> Then He said: A certain man had two sons. And the younger of them said to his father, "Father, give me the portion of goods that falls to me." So he divided to them his livelihood. And not many days after, the younger son gathered all together, journeyed to a far country, and there wasted his possessions with prodigal living. But when he had spent all, there arose a severe famine in that land, and he began to be in want. Then he went and joined himself to a citizen of that country, and he sent him into his fields to feed swine. (Luke 15:11-15)
>
> And he would gladly have filled his stomach with the pods that the swine ate, and no one gave him anything. But when he came to himself, he said, 'How many of my father's hired servants have bread enough and to spare, and I perish with hunger! I will arise and go to my father, and will say to him, Father, I

have sinned against heaven and before you, and I am no longer worthy to be called your son. Make me like one of your hired servants. (Luke 15:16-19)

And he arose and came to his father. But when he was still a great way off, his father saw him and had compassion, and ran and fell on his neck and kissed him. And the son said to him. Father I have sinned against heaven and in your sight, and am no longer worthy to be called your son. But the father said to his servants, "Bring out the best robe and put it on him, and put a ring on his hand and sandals on his feet. And bring the fatted calf here and kill it, and let us eat and be merry; for this my son was dead and is alive again; he was lost and is found." And they began to be merry. (Luke 15:20-24)

Both sons had been with their father, but one had been taken into the world, where he now had to contend with the things of the world by himself. Having journeyed to a far country, not knowing the costs that would be involved, the son would soon lose the inheritance that had been given him. Even the gifts which had been given him that were priceless—the love, the peace, the joy, the confidence, the morals, the values, the faith, the word, and even the protection would be taken. Everything would be gone.

When all the inheritance had been wasted, a severe famine had come, and he began to be in want. The thief had come to steal all that the younger son had been given, and now the thief was coming in for the kill, ever so slowly, but the enemy would wait for the condition to worsen. With everything gone, despair had made its presence known, and then shortly after this came frustration: "What am I going to do?" And then, came fear, panic, intimidation, doubt, humiliation: "What will I ever do?... Maybe if I do this, or maybe if I do this, or this, or this!! What can I do?"

Just as fortune would have it, he finds a job with a citizen of that country, who just happens to have an opening in the fields to feed the swine. He is broken down, frustrated, defeated, dismayed, feeling totally alone, and now even confused, for he is wondering how he had ever gotten to that point where he would even consider doing something which to his family was the lowest job anyone could have. Nevertheless, he takes the job. The thief had come in to steal who he was, kill his hopes and dreams, and was now ready to move in for the final kill—the destruction of his being.

What else was he to do! He had to live. He had to survive. They would only laugh at him back home if they knew how he had lost everything. His heart cried, but he was not going to let anyone know. Besides, he was in the fields, in the wilderness; no one would hear him, no one would care. But then, someone did hear him. Someone had been watching. Someone had cared, and the day came when he had a moment of sanity.

Jesus had come to pull him out of the prison where he was being held captive. Jesus had come to break through the walls that had been erected by the enemy. Jesus had come to destroy the weapons that were being used against him, and Jesus was coming to break into his spiritual prison. The prodigal son was able to remember where he had come from.

> I will arise and go to my father, and will say to him, "Father, I have sinned against heaven and before you."
> (Luke 15:21)

The prodigal son was going home. Upon seeing him, the father was so overjoyed that he was filled with compassion. He loved his son, but he knew that he had to let him go if he chose not to stay in his house. That no longer mattered, though, for now his son was back home. He had acknowledged that he had done wrong and that he had sinned, and that was good enough for the father. A festival would be held, for his son had come home. His son was no longer lost. His son was now found.

My brothers and sisters, there is absolutely no difference today. We all have been the prodigal son. Our Father is waiting for you to return home. I am deeply saddened every time that I see one of my brothers or sisters continue to battle with this very area, as they approach their own Jordan, for I know there is absolutely nothing I can say because it is God who must allow them to see the truth. So many are caught up in this trap!

Most do not realize that they truly have to do what is written in God's word, which says

> Put on the whole armor of God, that you may be able to stand against the wiles of the devil. For we do not wrestle against flesh and blood, but against principalities, against powers, against the rulers of the darkness of this age, against spiritual hosts of wickedness in the heavenly places. (Ephesians 6:11-12)

Good people are being herded back by the wiles of the devil! Good people who believe in God. Good people who are wanting and yearning for God. Good people who go to church. Good people who read God's word every day or every now and then. Good people who are being deceived.

WILES. Defined as tricks or stratagem intended to ensnare or deceive. Also, a playful trick. Trickery, guile.

STRATAGEM. Defined as a trick to deceive or outwit the enemy; also, a deceptive scheme. Skill in deception.

GUILE. Defined as deceitful, cunning. Duplicity.

DUPLICITY. Defined as the disguising of true intentions by deceptive words or action. (Definitions from the Merriam-Webster Dictionary)

I thought all of this might be of interest to you. These are power-packed definitions, all the way to duplicity. One leading to the other. One exposing a deeper meaning for the next to come, until the whole truth comes forth—*The disguising of true intentions by deceptive words or action.*

What a coincidence! This is exactly what Satan has been doing from the very beginning of time since the Garden of Eden. He has been disguising his true intentions by using deceptive words or action, *"WEAPONS"!!!!!*

This is no game. This is for real. Complete and total deliverance is a must, for without it, God's people will continue to battle with the same bondages, the very same weapons over and over again. Absolutely nothing can be hidden. There can be absolutely no cards under the table. It is a guarantee that the enemy will use them at the proper time to turn you back. It is time to look at just where you are. It is time to see just who you are. Are you headed to the other side, or are you still being held back on this side, to be returned to the wilderness?

God's message is so very clear. You are either for Him, or you are against Him. Do not be misled into believing that God does not make a choice. He has proved it in a number of ways. His own chosen people were allowed to be destroyed in the wilderness.

God will by no means give in to rebellion and disobedience. People need to begin making the decision to do what is necessary to lay aside every weight, including the sin which so easily ensnares them. God's love and concern for the sinner was indeed quite evident as Jesus described why it was so important to stay in His Father's house. Outside the Father's house, there is no rest.

> He who has ears to hear, let them hear. (Matthew 11:15)

◄ Today Is Your Day! ►

~ 15 ~

THE STORM IS PASSING BY

I give praise to the Father of our Lord Jesus Christ for the work that He is doing even today, for the grace which He allowed us to have, and for the spiritual gifts which He is bestowing upon His children, even without their knowledge.

Yes, my brothers and sisters, I am giving thanks for the mighty work that Our Lord Jesus Christ is doing within each and every one of you. A work the majority of you do not even know is happening, even at this very moment. For the storm truly is passing by, and the majority of you are not even aware, but that's okay, for Jesus has commanded this thing to happen, and it shall be done.

I believe that even today there has been an awakening in many of your hearts. An awakening to the truth, which is exactly what Jesus' purpose is. He has come to stir the hearts of His people. To stir His people to look unto Him who is:

> ...the author and finisher of our faith, who for the joy that was set before Him endured the cross, despising the shame, and has sat down at the right hand of the throne of God. (Hebrews 12:2)

Who even at the cross declared that what He had been sent to do, was now finished.

> So when Jesus had received the sour wine, He said, "It is finished!" And bowing his head, He gave up His spirit. (John 19:30)

The work of redemption had been completed once for all. Jesus had fulfilled what had been written. Jesus had fulfilled scripture. God is a God of stability, and what He had written would be done. Jesus had fulfilled what He had been sent to do and now was sitting at the right hand of the throne of God. This was His reward for being willing and obedient to do what God had called Him to do.

> Father, if it is Your will, take this cup away from Me; nevertheless, not My will, but Yours, be done. (Luke 22:42)

Yes, Jesus finished what He had been sent to do, and now His Holy Spirit remains within those who believe in His name to abide with them forever.

> The Spirit of truth, whom the world cannot receive, because it neither sees Him nor knows Him; but you know Him, for He dwells with you and will be in you. (John 14:17)

I truly believe that which I wrote earlier of there being an awakening in many of your hearts. For I truly believe that which is written in Matthew 10:34. "Do not think that I came to bring peace on earth. I did not come to bring peace but a sword." Loyalty. Loyalty to one side or to the other. The sword would separate the two, the double-edged sword, the word of God.

An awakening is coming to pass for many who have continued this far into this book; those who would not believe have stopped reading long ago, but those who have continued, who have pressed on, are those who from the very beginning have been called to receive the truth, and it is to you that Jesus is saying that the storm is passing!

> On the same day, when evening had come, He said to them, "Let us cross over to the other side." Now when they had left the multitude, they took Him along in the boat as He was. And other little boats were also with Him. And a great windstorm arose, and the waves beat into the boat, so that it was already filling. But He was in the stern, asleep on a pillow. And they awoke Him and said to Him, "Teacher, do You not care that we are perishing?" Then He arose and rebuked the wind, and said to the sea, "Peace, be still!" And the wind ceased and there was a great calm. But He said to them, "Why are you so fearful? How is it that you have no faith?" And they feared exceedingly, and said to one another, "Who can this be, that even the wind and the sea obey Him!" (Mark 4:35-41)

Let us cross over to the other side. (Mark 4:35)

Jesus had given the command. Jesus had known what was on the other side. He knew that on the other side there was victory, and they were going because God had commanded them to go, no matter what!

The disciples who were with Jesus were being commanded to cross over, for God had already made this part of His plan. The victory was going to be on the other side. Even though the disciples had no knowledge of what awaited them nor the purpose of this command. I am certain they were questioning within themselves what all this was about, although they knew that they would have to just be obedient. They knew that no matter what, they were going to go. No questions asked.

As I looked at this, I began to wonder just what was it that these disciples had that made them different, other than the fact that they were with Jesus, and the truth was brought forth—there was absolutely nothing different! These disciples were just people who had been called by Jesus to do a work that He had already planned for them to do. They were of different professions in life, which included fishermen, a lawyer, a tax collector, and others. They were all basically the same as anyone today would be. They were all human beings. They all made mistakes. They all had emotions. They were all just people who had been called—called to know the truth.

As I began to understand that there was no difference, I began to look at how tough it must have been to just go at a command, at a command that had to have stirred much uncertainty since they did not have any knowledge of just what they were being told to do. This is, without a doubt, a typical human reaction.

Nevertheless, they were going to go, maybe just out of curiosity—another famous human trait—but I am more swayed to believe that it was because all of this was already planned for their lives. They were going to be the ones who would be used by Jesus as an example that His love and mercy for His children was for real, that through them, we would be shown what we were to do.

Praise the Lord for that! For it is in this that Jesus is showing us that the storm is definitely passing by, and that we do not ever have to fear again. The hold of the enemy has been shattered, and the truth shall come forth, so allow Jesus to give you His peace as He shows you the way to the other side, as He shows you how and why you will cross with absolutely no fear, as He shows you why He said

> I am the way, the truth, and the life. (John 14:6)

> Now when they had left the multitude, they took Him along in the boat as He was. (Mark 4:36)

True victory sometimes requires a person to do things they are not accustomed to doing. The lame man being healed, of whom I wrote in an earlier chapter, is a classic example of this point. If the lame man had not looked up at Peter and John, he could have missed the greatest miracle in his life. The lame man had been caught up in his misery and in his rut for so long that it would have been very easy for him to continue in his ways. Had he not done what was told him, he would have without a doubt missed his miracle. How true that is in just about everyone's life! Sometimes a person will come to a point in their life where they will have to do something which is completely the opposite of what they would want to do.

"Now when they had left the multitude...." This is a separation from where they once were, a leaving behind of all that was before—even including people who have become part of our lives. Yes, there is going to be a time when you will have to leave the crowd behind. There is going to be a time when you will have to stop running with the crowd with whom you are accustomed. There is going to be a time that you will have to go it alone.

Crossing over is a decision that requires every single individual to look and evaluate their own life, and to do that which is required in order to get to the other side. This is something that cannot come to pass by asking your best friend what they think or by asking your social friends for their opinion, for there is absolutely no one who can know the giants you face in your life—no one except God and you. Only you can answer the questions which will arise from within you.

Crossing over is a very personal and individual decision and its outcome will be based on the decision you make. No one else can go for you, but just like the disciples in the boat, you can also be confident that Jesus will be in the boat with you as you cross.

And other little boats were also with Him. (Mark 4:36)

So many times I hear from brothers and sisters with whom I have shared the gospel, "You just don't understand my circumstances. You just don't know what I have gone through. If you only knew what I've gone through, you would know that it's not so easy taking the step which you are saying that I need to take."

People seem to think that they are the only ones who have gone through anything drastic, that their lives are the only ones that are being attacked, that their marriages are the only ones that are having problems, that their children are the only ones who are getting into trouble.

People seem to think that they are the only ones the boss ever seems to pick on, that they are the only ones the pastor doesn't seem to spend any time with, that they are the only ones who seem to be having trouble with their bills. The list goes on, and on, and on.

Well, all I have to say about all that is that it is time to open up your eyes and look around you, for the very same problems you are going through are basically happening to everyone else around you. You are definitely not the Lone Ranger in this area. Maybe most of the people do not want to admit it, but their lives are just as trying as everyone else's. The same battles that are being fought within you are being fought within everyone else.

Remember that the enemy uses the very same weapons over and over and over, on every single person. Satan just does not care who you are. What happens, though, is that he may use additional weapons on some that he does not use on others, depending on what he deems necessary to keep that person in bondage—weapons like causing the person to keep things to themselves so others do not know what is going on in their life, and then justifying it by saying that "Other people just do not care," or "It's none of their business." Satan is, without a doubt, very, very tricky.

As it is written in verse 36, "And other little boats were also with Him." There are others who have already gone through the very same things that you have, and just like you, Jesus is taking them across also. Believe me, with Jesus there are no cliques! With Him, you are going to have to cross over in your own little boat, as He leads you across! Therefore, my brothers and sisters, that "woe is me" attitude has got to go. There is absolutely no room in the boat for it. There is only enough room for you!

> And a great windstorm arose, and the waves beat into the boat, so that it was already filling. (Mark 4:37)

There is absolutely no joy in the storm, just like there can be no prosperity in the storm. The waves become quite violent at times, and can come up and try to sink you. You can be moving right along, and then all of a sudden, everything hits you all at once. The gas is going to be shut off, the light bill came telling you that you have until the next day to pay, bill collectors are calling every half hour, the food is all gone, the kids are fighting and screaming, you go to your car and the key breaks in the ignition, and everything that can go wrong goes wrong!

You lost your job, you are losing your house, divorce papers were served, the fighting has increased, the stress is overbearing. What more can go wrong! There is just no joy in the storm! It truly does seen like the water is filling the boat, and it feels like it is beginning to sink. There is just no prosperity in the storm! This is exactly why you need to go to the other side.

Jesus knows the weapons that are being used against you. He knows the windstorms in your life. He knows the waves that are beating against the boat. He knows when your boat is getting filled. This is why He said, "Let us cross over to the other side." *Us*, meaning you and Him!! He is taking you across. You are going to the other side, if you will allow Him to take you; nothing can stop you. Jesus has already told you that He would take you across; there is nothing that the enemy can do. Jesus has the victory, because He said so!

> But He was in the stern, asleep on a pillow. (Mark 4:38)

Imagine what the disciples must have been thinking about Jesus sleeping through the storm. How could He? How could anyone sleep through a storm? Jesus was showing us what it is that we must do when there is a storm in our life. Instead of reaching a state of panic and allowing the storm to overtake us as most people would do—and I was one of them—Jesus is telling us that we need to learn to rest while the storm passes by, that we need to ride the storm out and allow it to pass us by.

Jesus is telling us that we need to learn to look unto Him for only He can stop the storms, but during the storm you need to learn to rest while it passes by, and to believe that He is with you. You need to know that He is not shaken up by turbulence like man is, and that He will calm the waters.

It is time to begin confusing the enemy every time a storm comes up in your life by beginning to praise and thank Him for the peace He has given you, so that you can rest while He takes care of the storm. Believe me, the storm will pass you by!

> And they awoke Him and said to Him, Teacher do
> You not care that we are perishing? (Mark 4:38)

Again, it is time to begin confusing the enemy every time a storm comes up in your life by beginning to praise and thank Jesus for the peace He has given you, so that you can rest while He takes care of the storm.

All of us are guilty of having a faith that whines. Even the disciples did! "But Jesus, don't you care anymore?" "But Jesus, don't you love us anymore?" "But Jesus, can't you understand that I have a headache?" "But Jesus, can't you see that I'm too busy to pray?" "But Jesus, don't you…?" I think you get the picture! When we do not get our way, when it is not what we like, when we have to do something that we do not really want to do; it all has to come to an end.

Enough about whining though, I believe that we are all very familiar with it, but you do need to know that Jesus does care for you. He does care for the storms in your life. He does care that you are afraid. He does care if you sometimes feel like you are alone. He cared for you so much that He went to the cross for you, so that you could have victory over all the power of the enemy, and He is in the boat with you to make sure! He is going to take you across, if you will just allow Him to. Now not only does the "woe is me" attitude have to go, the whining has got to go, too!!

God does love you and He sent Jesus ahead to be in the boat with you. If you make the decision to let Him lead you, then you are going to the other side, no matter what. He is not shaken up with turbulence, storms, or waves, so you can rest. God knows exactly who is causing them, and has defeated him already!

> Then He arose and rebuked the wind, and said to the
> sea, Peace, be still. And the wind ceased and there
> was a great calm. (Mark 4:39)

Prior to receiving Jesus into my life, I can recall so many times from my past that things would happen to change a trial that I would be going through for the better, and I would not be able to explain it. Always my response would be, "It was just my luck that things went okay," or "It was meant to turn out that way," but in reality, I could not explain it.

Today, through this particular verse, I understand exactly what happened all of those times, in which I could not figure out why things just "happened" to work out.

When the Israelites were in the wilderness, God had always been with them to take care of them in all things. They were His people. Even though they were hard-headed and rebellious toward Him, He would continuously have mercy on them, no matter how much they complained or whined. He was always there to take care of them, even though they failed to see.

I see so clearly today that we are His people, and He is taking care of us in the exact same way, and we are just as hard-headed and rebellious as the Israelites were. I am so thankful that we have an even greater opportunity to know Him, through His Son, Jesus Christ, for it is He who continues to arise and rebuke the storm in our lives and says to the sea, "Peace, be still!" Because of it, the wind has to cease in our lives, and there is a great calm.

How I can recall those calm times in my life! They would always feel so good after going through the storms. What I did not know was to sleep through them though, and to get my rest while they passed. It's no wonder I was so confused; so many turbulent and choppy waters, and I didn't know what to do.

Today, I know! Jesus is the One who had been watching over me, and who caused the winds to cease, and who had created a great calm in the waters. Jesus is the One who allowed me to rest through the storms without losing it.

There is so much calmness in my life today. It is wonderful. Today I know that Jesus has given me the authority, through His name, over all the power of the enemy, and I can now rest through the storms while Jesus sleeps at the stern, and the very same awaits each and every one of you, if you will just allow Him to calm your storms. Praise Jesus! Once you know He is there, He is there always and will be there forever.

But He said to them, "Why are you so fearful? How is it that you have no faith?" And they feared exceedingly, and said to one another, "Who can this be, that even the wind and the sea obey Him?" (Mark 4: 40-41)

It is so important to know where Jesus is in your life, to know just where He stands. The disciples had seen Jesus perform many miracles, yet they were not certain how to perceive Him. "Who can this be, that even the wind and sea obey Him?" they asked. They were in awe but had not really received Him as the Son of God. Because of this, they resorted to fear because of the storm that was confronting them. The sad part was that most knew about storms already, for most were fishermen.

Jesus is very much aware of this problem. He knows that it is not an easy task for someone who has not known Him, to just all of a sudden believe. This is why it is so very important to know that God sent the Holy Spirit to guide us to the truth, which is exactly where faith comes in, for without it no one can ever experience the power of the Holy Spirit.

Faith is what will get you across. Faith is what will cause you to step into the waters and know that Jesus will carry you through. Therefore, faith must become a part of you if you expect to step across. Why? Because you still do not know where Jesus is in your life. Most people don't.

Many will say, "I believe in Jesus," but that is not what I am saying. You must know, without a shadow of a doubt, who He truly is and where He stands in your life. You must know the fullness of God, and you will. But for now you must depend on whatever faith you can muster up and trust that Jesus will do what He has said He will do.

Faith comes by hearing, and hearing by the word of God. (Romans 10:17)

Jesus was leading the way as He sat at the stern of the ship, and He still is leading the way! Where is Jesus in your life? Is He at the stern of your boat, or is He at the back, or maybe down in the galley?

There must be a hope of wanting to go across to the other side, even though you cannot envision it happening in your life. It will be this faith that will cause you to begin to look to Jesus and to know that you will be there because He said that your are going to the other side, no matter what—if you will just allow Him to steer your boat.

No matter what others say, or what they think, if Jesus said it, it is done, it is finished! Therefore, take that faith that God has given you and aim it at the situation. Allow God to be the pilot, and He will land you on the other side. You be the pilot, and the enemy will cause you to crash on this side, right before you are ready to cross.

What exactly has your faith done for you? Let your faith do something for you first, and then you will be able to do something for someone else. I assure you that once you cross over, you will know exactly what Jesus has done for you. No one will be able to tell you any different, for you will know.

Jesus' faith was in His command; "Let us go to the other side"! You need to believe what you say. Position your faith right, looking to Jesus who is the author and finisher of your faith.

> Commit your way to the Lord, trust also in Him, and
> He shall bring it to pass. (Psalm 37:5)

◆ Today Is Your Day! ◆

~ 16 ~

OUT OF DARKNESS INTO HIS MARVELOUS LIGHT

During the spring of 1993 the words, "out of darkness, into His marvelous light" came to my thoughts. At the time though, I did not know why. I had thought it could possibly be a title of the book God wanted me to write, something that never came about.

I knew though, that the words truly fit what He had done in my life almost an year earlier. He had definitely taken me out of darkness, and I had been placed into His marvelous light. I believed that if this was His purpose for me, then He would eventually reveal it to me again.

Almost two years had passed, and the words came up once again. This time my entire being was at a completely new level spiritually from where I had been when I first received these words. So many wonderful things were happening in my life. It had been almost three years since that glorious day in which Jesus came to set me free. I had experienced so many changes in my life during those three years; it was hard to imagine that God had just begun. The peace I was feeling inside was so wonderful! I had never known such an inner peace, and Jesus had made it all possible.

As the year 1995 began, I could not imagine what God had planned for my life. Just His having taken me to the point where I was as the year began was more than I could have ever dreamed. It was exciting to serve Him. I loved going to the prisons sharing what the Lord had done for me.

Every morning I remember getting up and asking God to use me in whatever way that He wanted to that day. I would ask Him to bring forth His spirit within me so that I might serve Him more effectively. I really did not know what I was asking for, as I am positive that He did not need me in order for Him to be more effective. Nvertheless, I just wanted to do whatever He wanted me to do. I owed Him so much. He had taken me from such pain and torment that no one can ever know unless they have been taken from the same.

For me, whatever way He chose for me to serve Him would have been okay. I simply wanted to share His gospel. I wanted to share what He had done for me. I wanted to share with others so they would not have to go through what they were going through anymore. God had brought me to such a point in my life that there was nothing I wanted to do more than to reach out to others with the Good News of Our Lord Jesus Christ. I simply wanted to serve Him and could see myself doing nothing more in my life.

Every single day I asked Him to produce more of His fruits within me, to produce more love, more peace, more joy, more longsuffering, more kindness, more goodness, more faithfulness, more gentleness, more self control. I had found that these were the only gifts worth having. They far surpassed anything that the world could offer me. I had tried it all. There was nothing that I wanted to have back.

And then a tremendous thing happened to me—something I would have never envisioned myself doing in my entire life. I had begun to have a very strong inner desire to preach God's word, a desire to become a minister of His word. Not a pastor of a church, but a minister of His word, an evangelist.

I went to my pastor and shared with him what I had been experiencing, and he replied what I had already known in my heart—that God had been speaking to me and was directing my life towards what He wanted me to do. Nevertheless, he encouraged me to continue to seek God in this decision, and he said that he would do the same.

I knew that the decision must be what God had determined. I had already told Him that I would do whatever He chose for me to do. Not quite two months went by when my answer came. At an almost identical time, Pastor Pete received his answer, and in March of 1995, I was licensed through Jesus Is Lord Ministries to preach the Gospel of Our Lord Jesus Christ.

Coincidence? Maybe. But I really do not believe so. In fact, I know that it was not. Through Pastor Pete, God had given a confirmation of what He had chosen for me to do. I was called to serve as an evangelist, not by a man, but by Jesus Christ. I consider myself to be one of God's boys, chosen by Him.

It was only a short time after being called by God to serve as a minister when exactly the same words that had been shown me two years earlier came to me. I was at work, and I was reading my Bible during break, when in my mind I began to see a design which had the words, "Out of Darkness" all around it. In the middle of the design were the words, "Into His Marvelous Light," and there were rays of light coming from the words. Then all the areas in which I had been held bondage during my life appeared within the light.

Alcoholism, drugs, hatred, anger, bitterness, prison, gangs. It was really quite an experience, for here I was seeing this entire design being formed in my mind. I could literally visualize the entire drawing. I was then led to begin drawing it out on paper, which I immediately began to do, and was amazed that the entire design was sketched within a fifteen-minute period.

As I sat there staring at what I had just drawn, it came to me what the words meant. I began to understand that the words were to be the name of the ministry which God had been preparing for me all along. You have to understand that I was very, very excited, for nowhere in my wildest dreams would I have ever imagined my becoming a minister to preach the Gospel of Jesus Christ, and to serve the Lord.

My life before had been completely the opposite from where Jesus was taking me now. My entire life had revolved around anger, hatred, shame, humiliation, alcohol, drugs, being a member of a very violent gang, and having spent a total of seven years in prison. Why would He pick me? Why would Jesus want to use a person who was completely opposite to what He stood for to do His glorious work? Why would he choose someone who was not educated and had been forever in trouble. Needless to say, I did not understand until He explained why.

What a simple answer it was! Actually it came in the form of a question. How else would I know what it was like to be imprisoned within, if I did not know myself? How else would I know about the weapons that were used by Satan to keep people captive, if I had never been held captive by them? Today I understand that I needed to know all of this in order for God to begin fulfilling the plan that He had for me from the very beginning of time. Today, I truly can say, thank you, Jesus!

After having sketched out the design, I got up and took it to a friend who worked with me, who just happened to be a freelance artist. Of course, this was just another coincidence. It also just happened that he was one of the persons with whom I had begun sharing what God had done for me two years earlier, after he came to me one day to tell me that he was impressed with how much I had changed in appearance. This, of course, opened the door and seemed like it had been planned all along. I told him about what I had just experienced and showed him the sketch I had been given.

As he looked it over, I explained what the drawing represented, and then I asked him if he could take it home and make the drawing look professional so I could take it to the printer and have it put on cards. He looked at me and said, "Ramón, I could not do anything to it. Everything is perfect the way it is." Needless to say, I was excited. Why? Because I had never drawn anything in my life. I was definitely no artist.

I went to another friend at work, whom I considered to be my spiritual mentor, as he always spoke to me about spiritual matters, and about things he had told me that God had shared with him to tell me, even though I did not understand them at the time. I shared with him what had happened in the break room.

About two hours later, this friend came to me, and told me that God had put it into his heart to pay for the cards, so to go ahead and have them printed, which I did! There was more that happened at the printers that was just as amazing, but I did not need to be shown anymore that God had ordained this drawing. This was a ministry that He was ordaining for me.

There are many exciting things that will happen to someone who is willing to follow Jesus. A few months later, while I was reading God's word, I came across a scripture which nearly floored me.

> But you are a chosen generation, a royal priesthood, a holy nation, His own special people, that you may proclaim the praises of Him who called you out of darkness, into His marvelous light. (1Peter 2:9)

Fortunately, I had been sitting at my kitchen table when I came across this scripture, for I was in a complete daze. God was once again showing me that He had ordained the work which I was doing. There was no question whatsoever in my mind that I had been called to do those things that God already had me doing. The foundation had been laid long before I arrived at this point. God was preparing me for His work, and today I know that He is just beginning to use me.

At that time I had been a three-year old babe in His service, and He was going through me like fire, burning out every little flaw from my old life, in order to prepare me for a new one. I would be on a mission in which the fire would continue to grow and grow, to become not just a more intense fire, but one that burned under His direction.

The beginning had occurred three years earlier, but the transformation would come only when He was ready to change me. I am so thankful today, for there is no greater bond one can have than that which the Lord Jesus Christ allows us to have with Him.

The words "out of darkness, into His marvelous light" were not written for just one person. They were written for all of the children of God who would be taken from darkness. Yes, they were written for the chosen generation, the royal priesthood, the holy nation, His own special people so that they could proclaim the praises of Him who called them out of darkness, into His marvelous light.

> Who once were not a people, but are now the people of God; who had not obtained mercy, but now have obtained mercy. (1Peter 2:10)

The new "Israel" now included believers who once were not a people and who had not obtained mercy.

You and I! Everyone who had never been included before. If any one thing should have meaning at all to you, it needs to be this very fact. You are part of the chosen generation, of the royal priesthood, of the Holy nation, of His own special people. And why? Because He loves you. Because of this, He is including you as one of His special people, so that you may proclaim the praises of Him who is calling you out of darkness, into His marvelous light. So that you may proclaim the praises of Him who has defeated the enemy in your life. So that you may proclaim the praises of Him who went to the cross to die that you could have victory.

Yes, you are being called out of darkness. Called out of it, before it has the opportunity to destroy you. Before the train has the opportunity to reach the end of the line.

DARK: being without light, gloomy, period of stagnation or decline, secretive.

LIGHT: Something that makes vision possible, daylight, enlightened, truth, particular aspect presented to view. (Merriam-Webster Dictionary)

Very simply put, the light wants you to know what is going on, and the darkness wants to keep what you need to know a secret—hidden. In order to accomplish this, the darkness puts into use weapons that are a part of the darkness to keep you from knowing the truth, to keep you distracted so you will never look to the core of the situation.

The enemy is well aware of the fact that if you become too curious, you will begin to investigate, and that would bring to light the truth about the darkness, which is what the enemy does not want you to know. Satan is very much aware of what was written in the word of God about the weapons he has been using to destroy the children of God.

> No weapons formed against you shall prosper, and every tongue which rises against you in judgment, you shall condemn. This is the heritage of the servants of the the Lord, and their righteousness is from Me, says the Lord. (Isaiah 54:17)

Do you really think that Satan wants this to get out? Weapons, weapons, weapons, "no weapons formed against you shall prosper"! And what exactly are these weapons? They are those very things which Satan uses to keep you in darkness, to keep you in a state of gloominess, to keep you in a period of stagnation, to keep you in a period of decline, to keep you from the light.

"This is the heritage of the servants of the Lord." Though His people will have to await the world to come for the beginning of this promise made in Isaiah 54:17, it still applies now. God foils evil plots and accusations made against His people.

My brothers and sisters, it is time to wake up. It is time to arise and shine! It is time to be released from the darkness. It is time to be released from the dungeons. It is time to be released from the inner spiritual prisons. It is time to allow Jesus to break through those walls which have kept so many in the dark.

> Arise, shine; for your light has come! And the glory of the Lord is risen upon you. For behold, the darkness shall cover the earth, and deep darkness the people; but the Lord will arise over you. And His glory will be seen upon you. (Isaiah 60:1-2)

Everything about the darkness and its weapons was written long ago. Yet the enemy would continue to shed doubt on God's word, so that God's children would never have the opportunity to find out, so that God's children would never have the desire to seek God's word, for Satan knew that only in this way would the truth be made known.

Weapons are used to injure, defeat, or destroy. They are a means of contending against another, to maintain in an existing state, to sustain against opposition, to assert. They are used to keep people in the dark, that they may never see the light until it is too late.

I must remind you that weapons used to keep people in the darkness can be, "adultery, fornication, uncleanness, lewdness, idolatry, sorcery, hatred, contentions, jealousies, outbursts of wrath (violent anger, rage), selfish ambitions, dissensions, heresies, envy, murders, drunkenness, revelries." These weapons include all works of the flesh found in Galatians 5:19-21, which also continues to say,

> ...of which I tell you beforehand, just as I also told you in times past, that those who practice such things will not inherit the kingdom of God. (Galatians 5:21)

Seriously, do you think that Satan really wants you to know this? Of course he doesn't. His whole purpose is to take you down with him. He does not want you to know that if you continue to rebel and to be disobedient to what He has instructed us not to do, that there is danger.

As I look back now at how bound I had been, I wonder how I could not have known. It is so obvious today as I look around at how few victories people have, compared to the defeats that they have. I was in a steady, continuous decline, a steady downhill spin. Every now and then I would have a victory, and I would feel good—always just in time before I really lost it. What a coincidence, just in time before I lost it! And it happened over and over again. How could I have been so blind?

I know now. I just did not know then. It was all part of the plan for destruction, all part of the plan to keep me in the wilderness until the train ran out of tracks, until the train got to the end, until the train crashed, and I was destroyed. It was all part of keeping me in the darkness so the light would never shine through with the truth.

Thank you Jesus, thank you for Your mercy. Thank you for allowing me to be one of Your children! Thank you for having taken me out of the darkness and having allowed me to be a part of Your marvelous light. God is light and in Him there is no darkness at all.

> ...this is the message which we have heard from Him and declare to you that God is light, and in Him there is no darkness. (1John 1:5)

My brothers and sisters, I am simply the messenger who has been sent to share the word with you. It is so important that you understand that the only thing that keeps one from God is sin. He said it, therefore, He obviously means it. "Those who practice such things will not inherit the kingdom of God." This scripture is so very, very clear. I know that there will be many who will say otherwise, but the fact remains that God will not say or do anything that is contrary to His word.

I lived in it. I know the bondage that was there. I know the darkness of the prison within. I know about the cold, ugly dungeons. I know about the obstacles that stood before me and that looked like giants. I also know about the weapons. I can assure you that they are what keep you in sin. They literally become the desires of the flesh.

The darkness of which God speaks, that there is none in Him, is sin. Sin is of the flesh, and God is spirit. Sin can have no part of the spirit; therefore, if one is to be a part of God, sin has got to go. Sin is the darkness. Sin is the lie. A person cannot continue with the ways of the world, and expect God to be on their side, to honor their prayers. He is telling us that we are either His, or we are not.

God in His word tells us that we have been freed from sin, if we choose.

> For he who has died has been freed from sin. (Romans 6:2)

This scripture is referring to the old man in us. The old man is the old person that we were before accepting Jesus into our life, what we had been before Jesus came to set us free. The old man has literally died, and the new creation has come to life.

> Likewise you also, reckon yourselves to be dead indeed to sin, but alive to God in Christ Jesus our Lord. (Romans 6:11)

Yes, we have been freed from sin and are brought to life in the new man, if we choose.

> For sin shall not have dominion over you, for you are not under law but under grace. (Romans 6:14)

This is so very, very powerful, and so very true. Sin shall not have dominion over you, for you are under grace, and that grace has been given to you by God.

> For by grace you have been saved through faith, and that not of yourselves; it is the gift of God. (Ephesians 2:8)

God has a plan for all of His children, but they must first choose Him. He is calling you out of darkness and into His marvelous light, if you will but hear. Do not be deceived into thinking that this does not include you. Remember that the enemy will use whatever he must in order to get you to turn back.

He will cause you to doubt as you are standing at the Jordan of your life, at the moment of truth, as you look out into the waters and across to the promised land. As you stand there wondering what you should do, as you stand there wondering if Jesus is really with you in the boat, as you stand there wondering if this is not just a dream.

My brothers and sisters, I can assure you that this is not a dream. He really is there. He is there and He is telling you to just trust in Him, as He has already given the command for you to cross. There is absolutely nothing that can stop you, but you. Everything else will have been an illusion, as you will find out, as you begin to step into the turbulent waters, and then there is a great calm. It will be then, and only then, that you will know that Jesus is for real.

Jesus has come to calm the storm! Jesus has come to lead the way! Jesus has come to lead you out of darkness and into His marvelous light, if you will but just allow Him, if you will but just choose.

> I have come as a light into the world, that whoever believes in Me should not abide in darkness. (John 12:46)

◄ Today Is Your Day! ►

~ 17 ~

TODAY REALLY IS YOUR DAY

My brothers and sisters, it has been a long journey, and I know that there have been many ups and downs, as we have traveled this path. This is without a doubt your day, though. The day in which you can now take a breather, while you begin to allow all of which you have received to sink into the innermost part of your being.

But that breather can be for only a moment though, as the enemy continues to lurk around like a lion waiting to devour; waiting for that opportunity to develop when he might sneak back in and break down all of what you have received. He is waiting for the opportunity to create doubt so he might turn you back—back to the wilderness, back to where he can continue to do that which has kept you in the clutches of his hands.

Only you know the cards that you are holding. It is now time to expose the hand that you have been playing with, for holding cards under the table can only open doors for the enemy to continue his dominance over you. Revealing all that you have is the only way to break any hold he may have. Believe me, Satan is trembling at this very moment, thinking that he has possibly lost you for good. Thank you, Jesus!

If you do not know Jesus, if He is truly not in your heart, then this is the day for you. This is the day which the Lord has made, this is the day in which you are to be set free! Now is the time to lay aside every weight and to begin to run the race that has been set before you, to lay aside anything that would hinder your progress, to search ever so diligently for any sin that may attempt to hide itself from you in order to attempt to entangle you at a later time.

If you are caught up in this trap, then free yourself today. Today really is your day. Today really is what you have been working for, today is what the truth has brought forth. Today, God begins to fulfill His plan for your life.

It is not where you came from that matters, but where God is taking you. Today I believe that He is preparing to do a great and mighty work in you. There is an appointed time and a due season for all to come to pass, if you will only believe and are willing to wait, to wait for His plan and His glory to come to pass.

The farmer who goes out to plant knows that there is an appointed time and a due season for a harvest. He knows that once the seeds are planted into the ground, it will be a few months before he can realize a harvest. He understands that if he does what is required of him in nurturing what he has planted and is willing to patiently wait for nature to take its course, then he will yield an excellent and fruitful harvest.

There is no in-between, there can be no short cuts. The farmer cannot simply go directly into the harvest if there is nothing to harvest. If the farmer neglected to plant his seed, there would be no harvest. Likewise, if the farmer planted the seed but did not nurture it and do what was needed so the seed might grow, there would not be a good harvest, for the majority of the crop would be choked out by weeds and would just die off. The very same holds true for you. What you sow, you will reap; good for good, bad for bad. Whatever you choose, the outcome or harvest of your life will be a direct result of what you sow.

There just can be no in-between. There just can be no short cuts. Absolutely nothing can be held back. There is a divine order in God's plan for man. If one is to know the fullness of God, the plan must be followed. It is time to begin cleaning house!

What really is there to lose if you just happen, and I mean just happen, to find yourself? Just happen to find the real you. Could it be possible that you just might feel good about losing all the bondage that has kept you from finding out who you really are? How sad to no longer feel the dreadful and painful things that have kept you locked up in your own personal prison, right?

Then again, maybe you really would not want to lose them. Maybe you want to continue to feel hurt, lonely, empty, afraid, bitter, angry, hateful, entrapped, controlled, envious, unclean, jealous, miserable, or whatever else you might want to hang onto, for there are people who have never known any other way, and they believe that this is the only way there is to live. I happened to be one of them.

But to you I say, how do you know if you would not like feeling free, if you never have truly been free? Not just the freedom that people are accustomed to which allows us to say, "I will be free on Monday to do this or that," but true inner freedom.

What would it be like if you did not feel hurt, lonely, empty, void, fearful, hateful, trapped, unclean, jealous, or miserable? What would it feel like to enjoy the other side, to be feeling peace in your life, joy in your life, love in your life? Again, not what the world would offer, but a true peace, a true joy, a true love. How great would you feel knowing that you are doing those things that you really want to do, and not doing those things that you do not want to do?

Where does one cross the line? Exactly where does one cross over? Just when or where does this happen? Can this really happen? Will this really happen? The answer to all of these should already be felt, but it is most definitely Yes! For those who choose to make this happen in their life, it will happen, but the decision must come from within you. No one else is able to make this for you, no one can make this happen unless you choose. Is it really worth it? All I can say is, you bet it is, just ask me!

I jump for joy each and every day; I jump, leap, shout, and give thanks every single day. Yes, it is most definitely worth it. No one could ever talk me into giving it back. As a matter of fact, I constantly request of Jesus to "give me more Lord, give me more"! No one knows exactly why, no one can really understand what has happened. Only I know what I have had lifted from me. No one can really know what happened to me that day when I cried out to Jesus—only me. I can attempt to describe it, but it would have no meaning to anyone else. People would be nice and say, "that's really nice," but it wouldn't mean anything to them. Soon they would forget about it. Why? Because it is not them.

Just like me though, others have known and others will know because they have already crossed over, or they will cross over that line. All I can say is that my life is different. I am different. I am excited about my life today. I am indeed grateful for my life today.

Only you can choose to make this happen in your life. Whether you are at the end and you have nowhere to turn, or your life is telling you that something must change, or you are just not sure, I encourage you to take a chance on the person who is within you. You are very much worth every effort you put forth for yourself. I encourage you to take a chance because there really is no other place to go. You've tried it all. You have tried to reach down deep within your being and have tried to dare yourself to make that decision in your life, but it just has never seemed to work.

My brothers and sisters, I can assure you that there is nothing to lose except the misery and bondage that has kept so many of God's children in captivity. God wants to take you and show you to the world. He wants to shape you, mold you, and discipline you to become what He wants you to be. He has a specific plan designed for each and every one of His children.

Satan has deceived God's children in such a great way that all they think about is their own problems, and because of it, they have no time to seek out the kingdom of God, but it is time to come out from all of this mess. It is time to arise from the ruts that the enemy has deceived so many to remain in for so long. It is time to get up, to get up from the problems that have overtaken your lives. It is time to stop worrying about what people will say about you.

If you are worried about people saying this or that about you, then stop worrying and begin rejoicing, for they said all that and more, and thought all that and more about Jesus first! They hated Him first, and that alone puts you in pretty good company!!

God's children are being mesmerized by the spirit of this age, by the wickedness of this age, by the darkness that is intensifying more and more with every day that passes. People are being herded into the wilderness with absolutely no comprehension of what is going on around them. It is time for God's people to find themselves and know just who they are, to stand up and begin to seek out what His plan is for them before they are taken to the end of the tracks, taken to their destruction.

If you want to know God's will for your life, first submit yourself to the known will of God (the Scriptures), and then the unknown will be made known to you. If one would simply be obedient to what He is saying to them in His known word, there would never be a need for one to have to make a decision in their life. Why? Because God has already put into order His divine plan, and all we need to do is follow it. Seriously, who needs decisions when all one needs is obedience!

But there are things which must be done before God can move in one's life. So many of God's people seem to always want to make a deal with Him; something to the effect of "God, if you will do this for me, I will do this for You." It would seem as if I may be guilty of having done this very thing, and of course I am!

Things on the outside will not change until you change what is on the inside. How you look at yourself determines what you will become, and you can change who you are and where you are by choosing. Choose to be hot or choose to be cold. Choose to be on one side or choose to be on the other, but at least make a choice, for Jesus can only work with you if you make a choice.

If you choose to be with Him, then you are way ahead. You will know His peace, love, and joy. If you choose not to be with Him, then you will still have all that you have right now, but at least Jesus will be able to cause a miracle to happen in your life, which may cause you to turn to Him before the train crashes.

But if you do not make a choice either way and remain lukewarm by trying to ride the middle of the fence, then Jesus will never be able to help you, for you will have hindered His working in your life. You cannot be on both sides. It has got to be either that you are wanting to cross over to the promised land, or that you refuse to cross over to the promised land. You cannot have a foot on both sides.

God is calling for us to get up. He is saying to us that He will set us free, and if He has said it, then I can assure you that He means it. We were not created to be deceived. We were not created to live in bondage. We were created in His image, which is why God has given us the opportunity through His Son Jesus Christ to know not only salvation in our lives, but deliverance from what the enemy has placed on us.

Salvation is for everyone who accepts Jesus as their personal Lord and Savior and believes that He died on the cross for them, so that they might have eternal life. Deliverance is for everyone who trusts in Him to do all that He has promised to do for them and surrenders completely to His will.

Salvation is indeed very, very important. Without it, it is impossible to ever know deliverance in one's life, simply because deliverance requires one to completely trust in Jesus to get them to the other side—to trust Him to do all that He has promised to do. Salvation, on the other hand, requires that one repent and accept Jesus as their personal Lord and Savior. If one does not repent and receive Jesus, then that means that they do not believe in Him, and obviously would never trust in someone whom they did not believe.

But can one have salvation and not deliverance? The answer to that is "most definitely!" As a matter of fact, many of God's children have absolutely no idea of what deliverance means, and the reason for this is that Satan has kept it hidden from them. Many of God's children have repented, acknowledged that

Jesus Christ died on the cross for them, and have asked Him to be Lord and Savior in their life, which is fantastic, but that is where it has ended! Many have been led to believe that this is all that was required of them, believing in Him, but I am saying to you that there is more. There is so much more. It is written,

> Jesus answered and said to him, Most assuredly I say to you, unless one is born again, he cannot see the kingdom of God. (John 3:3)

One must be born again, or simply put, there has to be a complete transformation from what one used to be, a complete turnaround, a total change. Everything from the old has got to be left behind, nothing can be kept. It is more than simply being saved, it is becoming a new creation.

> Therefore, if anyone is in Christ, he is a new creation; old things have passed away; behold all things have become new. (2Corinthians 5:17)

Of course, Satan wreaks havoc with God's children on this issue. He knows that if he is able to get them to just believe that they are saved, they will miss the rest. They will miss the understanding that there must be a complete turnaround, a total change. Why would Satan want to get God's children to focus on the fact that they are saved? Well, now it gets really interesting! I had thought it strange that Satan would get people believing that they were indeed saved, even more strange that he allowed scripture to back it up, and then one day Jesus made it clear to me: What better way to keep people from crossing over than to get them to believe that they already have?

Why? Well, if Satan did not create confusion in this area, people would be looking to the other side. That would mean that they would be getting an understanding of what deliverance is all about, and if they had knowledge of this, they would be on the other side, and if they were on the other side, then they would be a new creation, and if they were a new creation, then they would be a thorn in his side!

I am not trying to confuse you with this. Just follow along, and it will be made clear. Jesus desires for all to be exposed. Especially when God's Word has been used to deceive us. Therefore, do not get bogged down trying to analyze what is being said. I assure you that you will see clearly the deception.

Now, this is something he could not afford to let happen, for then those who have been delivered or transformed from who they were would be walking under the authority of Jesus Christ and would be going out into all the world preaching the gospel as Jesus has commanded us to do, with the power of the Holy Spirit, to all nations. They would be exposing the lies and deceptions that are being used to keep God's children in captivity so they will know the truth.

Of course, we all know that Satan would not be very happy about all that, so what does he get them to do? He gets them to believe that which is said in the Bible. And what is that? That they will be saved, and of course they will, for God cannot lie. But here is the catcher: *If they make it!*

My brothers and sisters, Satan is gambling that he will get you, before you know what is going on. He is taking the chance that he will defeat you before that happens, and to answer the question "how could one not make it?" please allow me to tell you.

God loves His children, and He wants all of us to be with Him. He sent His only Begotten Son to die on the cross just to prove it. Now, here we have His children holding firm to His word that they will be saved if they will only believe in His Son Jesus. But now, Satan comes in and gets you to focus on that particular point, to focus on the fact that God's Word states that you will be saved if you will just believe, and it really does say this. Believe me, people will argue forever on this point.—anyone want to take a stab at why?

Having accomplished that confusion, Satan now begins to cloud the part of being born again, the part of the transformation. The part of the change that must come about, the part of the new creation—all brought to pass by using weapons which will keep your attention focused on what is happening in your life and away from the truth, away from the fact that Jesus said that "one must be born again"! So you continue to go through life, never making that change, never having known what God has promised to you in His word, never having known true freedom, never having known deliverance, and all because Satan deceived you with what you wanted to hear—that you were saved.

Just ask all those who are walking around claiming salvation, but living in darkness. And guess what? In order to claim salvation, they must first have been believers! But walking in darkness! It is time to look at the truth. For in reality, all they have accomplished is to have remained in the wilderness, deceived into believing that they were okay, but never having known the truth of what they were supposed to have done to gain deliverance into the promised land.

Something is wrong. Something is desperately wrong!

What is wrong is that by never having crossed over to the other side, by never having been born again, by never having had a complete transformation from the old to the new, they have been a wide open target for Satan's weapons, all along believing that they were saved.

And then it hit me!

As long as Satan has you on that side, he continues to have dominance over you, and as long as he has dominance over you, he has the opportunity to eventually wipe you out. He is very much aware of the fact that if you were to cross over, he could not do anything to you, for you would know the truth about him and his plan. That is why it is important for him to keep you in the dark if he is to have the opportunity to eventually wipe you out, *before Jesus returns*. Of course if he succeeds, it will then be too late for you.

It will have been like the Israelites in the wilderness, God's people. They were continuously being deceived, continuously being tricked. Into doing what? Into being rebellious and disobedient to what God had instructed them to do. Because they were always too busy doing those things that were important to them, their attention was manipulated so that they would never focus on the instructions God had given them in His Word! The end result: God would not allow them to cross over to the promised land, and all because of their continuous rebellion and disobedience. No matter what, we are still held accountable for what we do.

Satan has been doing this all along. Generation after generation, the children of God are being deceived, simply so Satan can fulfill his plan of destruction.

Jesus said that one must be born again. He has said that there must be a change. He has said that there must be a transformation. This can only be accomplished by trusting Him to fulfill His promises to you

> Then they cried out to the Lord in their trouble, and
> He delivered them out of their distresses. (Ps 107:6)

Yes, God is indeed ready to deliver any of His children who cry out to Him and are willing to surrender to His will completely, for then He is able to fulfill His plan for their life, ready to deliver all those who are willing to trust Him. This is no game. Satan is out to steal, and to kill, and to destroy! He just does not care! By ourselves, we are no match for him.

Remember that the enemy will do whatever it takes to keep you from crossing over to the other side. He cannot afford to have you there, for then you, too, just might become a pain in his side. Even though he will try to get you to believe that it is different now, that it is not the same as it was back then, *do not believe it!* There is absolutely no difference!

Either one is obedient to what God has instructed them to do, or they are disobedient to what God has instructed them to do. Do not be deceived into thinking otherwise.

My brothers and sister, there is but one way to go. I have attempted to share what Jesus has wanted me to share with you in this book, so that you would begin to see the truth of what the enemy is doing, the lies, the deceptions, the inner spiritual prisons. It is time to be set free. It is time to have the light shine in. It is time to have Jesus become Lord and Savior of your life. It is time to allow Him to take you across to the other side. It is time to allow Him to calm the waters in your life.

> I am the Way, the Truth, and the Life. No one comes
> to the Father, except through me. (John 14:6)

There is only one way to go. Jesus died on the cross so that His children might have eternal life. Right now, I ask you to take a few moments to think about where you are with Jesus, to think of just where you have Jesus in your life., to think if you have even considered Jesus as part of your life!

Salvation comes through repenting, acknowledging your belief in the cross, and then accepting Jesus as your personal Lord and Savior. Right now I would say to you that if you do not know Jesus in your life, then today is your day. If you do not know where you are with Jesus, then today is your day. If you just are not certain, then today is your day. Today is your day to ask Him into your heart, and to ask Him to forgive you for not having known. Simply pray with me right now:

> *Father, forgive me for I have sinned greatly against You. I repent of all those things which I have done wrong against you. I repent for having hurt you. I understand today how I have been deceived into being rebellious and disobedient to Your word. Jesus, I do believe that You died on the cross for me, so that my sins would be forgiven, so that I could have eternal life with You. And I do believe that You rose from the dead and are now sitting at the right hand of the Father. And just like You have forgiven me, I also forgive all those who have done wrong against me. I do accept You as my personal Lord and Savior, and will trust in You from this day forth. I ask You right now to come into my heart, and to allow Your Holy Spirit to teach me what I need to know. Amen!*

That's it. If you were truly sorry and said this prayer with all your heart, then Jesus has heard you. I don't care what has been said to you by others, all has been forgiven. There is nothing too big for Jesus to take care of. You are forgiven! Jesus died for you! He did the will of His Father so that you would be forgiven, and if He did this great thing for you, than why would He not forgive you? But you must trust in Him to guide you across to the other side, and you must be willing for Him to begin changing you. This must happen.

Now for those who have received Jesus before, but never knew of just how Satan was deceiving you with the idea of being saved, I pray that you also said this prayer with all sincerity, for Jesus has known your plight. Jesus has known how Satan has deceived you. Therefore do not allow Satan to continue to deceive you. Get rid of that pride that I know is holding so many of God's children in severe bondage. Remember that pride will hinder God from working in your life.

No matter what, today is your day for salvation. Today is your day for deliverance.

> *Satan, in Jesus name you are defeated. In Jesus name, all those who have seen the light, and now know the truth, are now set free. No more will you use this weapon against them! Amen.*

I speak to all nationalities, all denominations, and all religions, regardless of whether you have believed in Jesus before or have never done so. I speak to those in ministry and to those not in ministry.

Confusion and discord are not of God. Still, this is exactly what controls our world today. This is exactly what controls the people today. This is exactly what controls the denominations today. This is exactly what controls the religions of our world today.

It is time to have the scales removed from our eyes, and to see that we are all fighting the same fight. We are all fighting the same enemy. The enemy is not you or I. It is not this nationality or that nationality. It is not this religion or that religion. It is not this denomination or that denomination. We all have the same enemy, and the same identical weapons are being used against every single one of us by the ruler of this age—Satan!

It is time to wake up! It is time to arise and shine! It is time to reach our hand out to our brothers and sisters, and to help them get out of the rut that they have been in for so long. It is time for each and every one of us to share the truth with those who are still in bondage, for without you, your families and friends may be destroyed for lack of knowledge. Once again, take the time to look around you. Nothing really needs to be said if you know what you are looking for. Obviously, Satan has not wanted any of this to be made known, or there would not be all of this confusion, turmoil, and destruction in our world. There would not be all of this discord among the people. There would not be all of this division in the church.

Take the time to seriously look around you. Take the time to seriously examine your life. Take the time to seriously look into your inner being. Take the time to listen to the little child who is trapped within you. Take the time to allow Jesus to set the child free. Do not allow yourself to be trapped by the religious spirit that is out to destroy. Do not allow yourself to be trapped by traditions, views, and doctrines of man. Allow Jesus to give you your answers.

I urge you to contact someone who has full understanding of what deliverance means—as soon as you can. Do not wait. It is that important. Find a church that is on fire for Jesus. Salvation is the beginning. Now deliverance must follow. Now you must allow Jesus to lead you across to the other side. You need the power of the Holy Ghost. Satan will not quit just because you have decided to cross over. He will do whatever he has to in order to get you to turn back, but that's okay, for there is nothing that he can do against you, for Jesus is leading the way.

If you are unable to find a place you can turn to, if you have any questions about Out of Darkness Ministries, or if you wish to inquire about bookings for speaking engagements, please feel free to contact me at the following address, phone, fax, or e-mail:

> Out of Darkness Ministries
> Ramón Saenz
> P. O. Box 591
> Adrian, MI 49221-9810
> Office (517) 265-1564
> Fax (517) 265-6057
> E-mail odm@tc3net.com

You can also visit our web site at:
www.lenaweb.com/outofdarkness

May the blessing of the Lord be upon each and every one of you as you begin to reach down into the very core of your inner being to take that first step, as you begin to take that step into the turbulent waters of your own Jordan, your own moment of truth!

*Allow Jesus to begin
Breaking into Your Spiritual Prison*

◄ **Today Really Is Your Day!** ►